THE

FIFTH LETTER

OF

HERNAN CORTES

TO THE

EMPEROR CHARLES V

CONTAINING AN

ACCOUNT OF HIS EXPEDITION TO HONDURAS

Translated from the Original Spanish

BY

DON PASCUAL DE GAYANGOS

INTRODUCTION.

THE fifth letter of Hernando Cortes to the Emperor Charles V, describing his expedition to the bay of Honduras, has never, to our knowledge, been turned into English. In 1843, a citizen of the United States translated* the second, third, and fourth—the only ones published during the conqueror's lifetime, and often reprinted since; but of the first and last in order no satisfactory account could then be given, as they had long been missing, and had not yet appeared in the original Spanish. Robertson was the first to suspect that they might possibly be ·discovered in some of the archives at Vienna, the Emperor Charles being in Germany when one of them reached Europe. And so it turned out to be, for in a manuscript volume of the Imperial Library, marked CXX, an attested copy of the former was found, of which that diligent historian soon published an abstract.† Along with it, in the same volume, was Cortes' fifth letter, or *Carta quinta de*

* "The Despatches of Hernando Cortes, the Conqueror of Mexico, addressed to the Emperor Charles V." By George Folson. New York, 1843, 8vo.

† "History of America." Notes and Illustrations, xcvii.

relacion, which we now give in English for the first time.

Of the missing letters, the first, dated July 10, 1519, wherein an account is given of the conqueror's first landing at Veracruz, and of his subsequent progress into the country, was first published* in 1844, by the learned and much regretted Navarrete. The fifth appeared soon† after ; and since then both have been reprinted, first by Don Enriqué de Vedia in Ribadeneyra's *Biblioteca de Autores clasicos,*‡ and afterwards by the present translator.§ Doubts, however, have been entertained about the first of these letters, some critics asserting—not without foundation—that besides the *Relacion,* which, though signed by Cortes himself, appears addressed to Charles V by the *Justicia y Regimiento* of Veracruz, or in other words by the municipal corporation of the town newly founded by him : there must have been another—perhaps, too, a fuller one—sent to the Emperor in the conqueror's own name, as commander of the small force that set foot on the shores of the Mexican empire. The facts stated in either must have been substantially the same; and yet such were the magnitude and importance of the undertaking, and the peculiar turn of the hero's mind, that it

* "Coleccion de Documentos inéditos para la historia de España," vol. i, pp. 421-61.

† Vol. iv, pp. 1-167.

‡ "Historiadores primitivos de Indias," tom. i, 1852, vol. xx, pp. 1-153.

§ "Cartas de Hernan Cortes al Emperador Carlos V." Paris, 1866.

makes us regret that this portion of his own personal narrative has been lost.*

But if objections have been raised against the text of the first *Relacion,* it is not so with regard to the fifth, the most important of all in a geographical point of view; for if we only cast a glance at the map of that portion of central America traversed by Cortes in his route to Honduras, we cannot but admire his chivalrous spirit—not uncommon in that age—his undaunted and patient courage in moments of danger and privation, his aptitude for command and other qualifications for such an adventurous undertaking. With a handful of men, with no other assistance but that of a small compass, and of a very imperfect map furnished him by the natives of Tabasco, marking the principal places visited by Indian traders in their wanderings over those wild regions; with such guides as from time to time he could pick up in his journey, Cortes traversed that broad and level tract which forms the base of Yucatan, and spreads from the Coatzacoalco river to the head of the gulf, called by the Spaniards of those times Golfo de las Hibueras, and now known as Bay of Honduras—thus performing one of the longest and most perilous marches ever attempted in ancient or modern times.

* Gonzalez Barcia, who was the first to reprint the three letters (second, third, and fourth), was of opinion that the one written by Cortes after his landing at Veracruz was perhaps the same that the Council of the Indies is said to have suppressed at the request of Pamphilo de Narvaez, or that which Juan de Flores took from Alonso de Avila.

The causes that brought on and determined Cortes' expedition are well known. It was a common belief among Spaniards of that time—and principally among those who, impelled by a spirit of adventure, left their country for the New World—that the Pacific was no other than the far-famed Indian Ocean, studded with golden isles, and teeming with the rich treasures of the East. Cortes, like most Spaniards of his day, firmly believed in a strait which should connect the two seas, and his letters to the Emperor are filled with this favourite idea, which he seems to have cherished to the last day of his life. "Most of all," does he say in one of his letters[*] to the Emperor, " do I exult in the tidings lately brought me of the Great Ocean ; for in it, as cosmographers and those learned men who know most about the Indies inform me, are scattered innumerable isles teeming with gold and pearls, abounding in precious stones, as well as in spices, and where, I feel confident, many wonderful secrets and admirable things may be discovered."[†] Again, in 1524, he wrote : " Your Majesty may be assured that knowing, as I do, how much you have at heart the discovery of this great mystery of the seas, I shall postpone all interests and projects of my own—some of them of the highest moment—for the fulfilment of this great object."

Accordingly, no sooner had he entered Mexico for the second time, than he fitted out two expeditions,

[*] " Tercera Relacion," ap. Lorenzana, p. 302.
[†] " Quarta Relacion," *ib.*, p. 385.

which, after reaching Mechaocan, penetrated to the borders of the Great Southern Ocean. No European had yet descended on its shores so far north of the equator. They visited on their return some of the rich districts towards the north, bringing samples of gold and pearls from the Gulf of California.

Another expedition fitted out at Zacatula, in the Gulf of Mexico, and destined to the coast of Florida, was equally successful; and though the wonderful passage that was to connect the two seas was not found, the always increasing reports of the fertility of the land and the richness of its mines confirmed Cortes in his belief, and made him more eager than ever to discover the "great mystery of the sea," as he often calls it in his letters to the Emperor.

For this purpose he prepared another and larger squadron, and giving the command of it to Christoval de Olid—the brave officer who commanded one of the divisions of the besieging army—instructed him to steer for Honduras and form a colony on its northern shore. This being accomplished, a detachment of his squadron was to cruise along its northern shores towards Darien, and look out most diligently for the mysterious strait. About the same time Alvarado terminated the important conquest of Guatemala, thus extending the limits of the conquest, and increasing the geographical knowledge of those seas.

Olid, however, turned out unfaithful. Having touched at La Havana, he was there persuaded by Velasquez, the bitter enemy of Cortes, and at the

time more enraged with him than ever,* to strike
out for himself and proclaim independence. No
sooner, therefore, had that officer reached his destination and made a settlement on the adjoining coast,
than he shook off his allegiance to Cortes—under
whose orders he was acting, and with whose treasure
the expedition had been fitted out—publicly declaring that he would hold his conquest in the
Emperor's name, without any subjection to his com-
mander-in-chief. And not only did he thus rebel
against Cortes' authority, but hearing that some
Spaniards under Gil Gonzalez Davila, coming from
the Western Islands, had settled higher up the
coast, he sent against them part of his force and
took their leader prisoner. Francisco de las Casas,
a kinsman of the conqueror, was dealt with in a
similar manner. On the news of Olid's rebellion
reaching Mexico, Cortes had dispatched him at the
head of a small force in three vessels, with orders
to seize the person of his rebellious lieutenant and
bring him to his presence; but after some fighting,
which ended in negociation, the vessel on board
of which Las Casas was, struck on a rock, and was
wrecked on the shore; upon which Olid—who from
the beginning was treacherously inclined, and had
only consented to treat with a view to gain time—
seized the opportunity, and took him prisoner.

* Some time previous to this event the influence of Bishop
Fonseca, one of the members of the Council most opposed to
Cortes, had ceased to be felt at court, and the long-pending suit
between him and Velasquez had been decided in his favour.

Shortly after, however, Gonzalez Davila and Las Casas, who had been allowed to move freely about the camp, joined in a conspiracy against the usurper —whose tyranny and arrogance had become intolerable even to his own men—and having with the assistance of their numerous partisans surprised Olid in his own dwelling, secured his person, had him tried by court-martial, and publicly beheaded him at Naco.

Of these late proceedings Cortes had no knowledge whatever. No tidings of the death of Olid and of Las Casas' ultimate success had reached him; and although he had every reason to trust in the loyalty of his kinsman and lieutenant, he must have had serious misgivings about the fate of the expedition under his orders. On the other hand, were Olid's defection to remain unpunished, the most mischievous consequences might be apprehended for the future, as it would prove a dreadful blow dealt to his authority in the newly conquered land. He therefore determined to go to Honduras himself; he might thus be able to ascertain from personal inspection the mineral resources of the country, and perhaps discover that point of communication between the two seas which his lieutenant had been unable to find, and which he still felt confident was reserved by Providence to his own exertions. Accordingly, on the 12th October, 1524,* Cortes left Mexico with

* There can be no doubt about this date, and yet there are letters of Cortes to the Emperor, dated Mexico, 13th and 15th of October, in the latter of which he informs him that *he has de-*

about four hundred Spaniards and three thousand Indian auxiliaries, taking with him the proud but unfortunate Guatemozin—who was to meet with his death on the road—and several other Mexican chiefs. He was accompanied by Gonzalo de Salazar, the factor, Pero Armildez Chirinos, the veedor or royal inspector, and other crown officers. The administration of justice and the government of the country he left in the hands of the treasurer, Alonzo de Estrada, and of the accounting-master (contador), Rodrigo de Albornoz, assisted by a lawyer named Alonzo de Zuazo. No sooner, however, had he reached the town of Espiritu Santo, when news came to him of serious disturbances in the capital, owing to his lieutenants having quarrelled among themselves; and, though he immediately provided for the emergency by sending back in all haste Salazar and Chirinos to take the government of the city into their hands, this was not accomplished until some months after, when much blood had been shed, and a rival faction created, which ever after was hostile to Cortes and to his administration.

sisted *from his intended expedition to Honduras.* This difficulty, however, has been overcome by Garcia Icazbalceta, in his recent *Coleccion de Documentos para la historia de Mexico,* p. 41—a work of much research, and where many an interesting paper has been published for the first time—by surmising that Cortes really left on the 12th, and encamped in the outskirts of the city for some days, but went on dating his letters from Mexico, a practice not at all uncommon in those times. It is not so easy to determine what reasons he had to make the Emperor Charles V believe that he abandoned his idea, when he evidently was more intent than ever on its prosecution.

Notwithstanding the anxiety which such news must have caused him ; notwithstanding the almost incredible fatigues and dangers of a march through unknown regions, inhabited by wild Indian tribes ; Cortes, with a resolution and a steadiness of purpose that cannot be sufficiently praised, accomplished his object, and, after an absence of nearly two years, returned to Mexico, where new disturbances had broken out.

To determine the spots visited by him in this extraordinary march through almost impenetrable forests, swampy plains, or lofty mountains, has by some writers been pronounced a hopeless task ;* and though we possess the narrative of that stout-hearted and sturdy soldier Bernal Diaz, who formed part of the expedition and carefully noted down its principal events ; though the various provinces traversed by the devoted army have since been more or less explored by travellers of all nations,† few are the in-

* Mr. Prescott, among others, despaired of ever accomplishing it. "I have examined," says he, "some of the most ancient maps of the country by Spanish, French, and Dutch cosmographers, and I can detect on them only four or five of the places indicated by Cortes." *Conquest of Mexico,* book vii, chapter iii ; see also Stevens' *Incident of Travel.*

† About ten years ago, an enterprising French traveller, Mr. Arthur Morelet, published two volumes of travels in these remote regions. Starting from Havana, in the island of Cuba, and landing at Sisal, on the western coast of Yucatan, he travelled by land from Merida to Campeachy, entered the Laguna de Terminos, ascended the river Palizada until it joins the Uzumazinta, and proceeding afterwards in an eastern direction, traversed the continent to Flores on the lake Itza, crossing on his route the rapides de Tenosique and the river Yalchilan. Bending then

dications—and those very slight—of the route they followed. He must have passed near the ruins of Palenque, since the small village of Las tres Cruzes is said to derive its name from three wooden crosses left in that locality. We know also that he crossed the *Sierra de los Pedernales* by a most dangerous pass, to which he gave the name of *Puerto del Alabastro*, and that after a march of five days through districts more or less inhabited, he reached a large lake, which appeared to him to be an arm of the sea, but could be no other than the Laguna de Peten, or Itza, as it is otherwise called, in the country of the Lacandones, the most warlike nation of those parts. He seems to have visited the Indian town in the middle of the lake, and destroyed the Indian teocallis or temples on it, leaving unequivocal traces of his passage. Lastly, the situation of the two towns Naco and Nito, where the wretched and half-starved relics of former expeditions were found, is equally ascertained. But beyond these few places, on an extent of country calculated at one thousand miles, we hardly know which is the precise route followed by the conquerors. They must have crossed more than once the Rio de San Pedro, perhaps, too, the Uzumazinta,* across one of which rivers

towards the south, he visited Santiago de Guatemala and Iztapan, and making for the lake Yrazabal and Golfo Dulce, returned by sea to La Havana. He must thus have gone through a portion of the country traversed by Cortes, and yet either he had no knowledge of this letter, or else he could not identify any of the spots named by the conqueror in his narrative.

* This river has its source in the mountains of Peten, not far

Cortes himself informs us a bridge was thrown measuring 934 spans in breadth. Indeed, though the native writers tell us that some of these bridges were still standing many years after, and were generally known as *Las Puentes de Cortes*, they have neglected to say the precise spot on which they stood, thereby increasing our perplexity and doubt in this matter. Neither is Cortes' narrative as clear and connected as might have been expected, being evidently drawn up some time after his return to Mexico, and when some of the events of a march so fraught with dangers of all kinds, as well as the names of Indian localities and chiefs on his passage, may have escaped his memory.

To those English readers who take an interest in geographical discovery, and who know how imperfect our knowledge has hitherto been, and is still, of the regions traversed by Cortes in his wonderful march across Central America, the translation of this letter —in every respect one of the most interesting he

from San Luis. It runs first in a south-western direction under the name of Santa Isabel, and mixes its waters with those of another considerable river called Lancontun. Flowing then towards the north with increased rapidity, it takes the name of Rio de la Pasion, and again at Tenosique, the last village in the province of Tabasco, resumes its old name (Uzumazinta). Crossing there the imposing chain of mountains that separates Mexico from Central America, it branches out into three rivers, the most western of which preserves its name until it mixes its waters with the Grijalva, above La Frontera. The other two are known as San Pedrito and Palizada, and all empty their waters into the Mexican Gulf. *Voyages dans l'Amérique Centrale, l'Ile de Cuba, et le Yucatan.* Paris, 1857, vol. ii, p. 23.

ever addressed to the Emperor—cannot fail to be acceptable. We have carefully noted down the various readings afforded by the only two copies known to be in existence, the Vienna one, already alluded to, and another one which Don Juan Bautista Muñoz, the historian, saw in the National Library at Madrid. Neither of them, in our opinion, is sufficiently correct, since they scarcely once agree as to the writing of proper names, already very much corrupted by the conquerors themselves; yet we are inclined to give the preference to the latter, if, as asserted, it was made upon the original of Cortes by Alonso Diaz, one of his officers.

FIFTH LETTER OF HERNAN CORTES.

MOST SACRED MAJESTY :—On the 23rd day of the month of
October of the year 1525 past, I dispatched from the town
of Trujillo, off the port and cape of Honduras, to the
Hispaniola, a vessel, and in her a servant of mine, with
orders to pass over to those kingdoms of Spain. The said
servant was the bearer of letters, wherein I informed your
Majesty of some events which had occurred at the gulf
called Las Hibueras[1] between the two captains[2] I had sent
thither and another captain named Gil Gonzalez, who went
afterwards. And as I was unable at the time the said vessel
and messenger departed, to give your Majesty any account
of my journey and adventures, from the moment I left this
great city of Tenuxtitlan until I met with the people of
those distant parts, it seemed to me important that your
Highness should become acquainted with my doings, were
it only for the sake of not failing in my invariable custom,
which is to advise your Majesty of all things wherein I am
concerned. I will therefore narrate events plainly and to
the best of my ability, because, were I to attempt drawing

[1] The name of this gulf is variously written—Higüeras, Higueras, etc.;
but Herrera and Juarros, both good historical authorities, call it
Hibüeras, which in the dialect of the country means " pumpkins," from
a species abounding in that locality.

[2] These were Christoval de Olid and Francisco de las Casas.

them in their proper colouring, I am sure I could not do it, and, moreover, my narrative might perhaps be unintelligible to those for whom it is destined ; and will relate only the principal and most remarkable incidents of the said journey, passing over in silence many others, as accessory, which might also have furnished ample matter for much writing.

Having taken my measures in the matters concerning Christoval de Olid, as I wrote to your Majesty,[1] I began to consider how long I had been inactive, and without undertaking things that might be of service to your Majesty ; and although my arm was still sore and painful,[2] I determined upon doing something useful. I therefore left this great city of Tenuxtitlan[3] on the 12th day of October of the year 1524 last, followed by a few horse and foot, chosen among my own retainers and servants, and by some friends and connexions of mine. In this number were Gonzalo[4] de Salazar and Peralmindez Chirino,[5] the former a factor, and the latter a veedor of your Majesty. I likewise took with me the principal among the natives of the land ; and left the administration of justice and the government of the country in the hands of Alonso de Estrada and Rodrigo de Albornoz, the treasurer and accounting-master of your Majesty, conjointly with the licenciate Alonso de Zuazo. I provided this[6] city with the necessary artillery, ammuni-

---

[1] In his letter to the emperor, dated from Tenuxtitlan, 15th of October, 1524, Cortes announced his determination to go in search of his rebellious lieutenant.

[2] No doubt from the wound received during the siege.

[3] Generally written Temixtitan, Temixtiltan, or Tenestutan ; frequently also Tenuxtitlan, as in the text, which reading I have adopted as most resembling Tenochtitlan, which I believe to be its real Aztec name.

[4] The Vienna copy says Agustin, which is a mistake.

[5] The name of this individual, who was *veedor*, *i. e.*, surveyor or inspector, is variously written, throughout Cortes' correspondence, Peralmildez, Pero Armildez Chirinos, and Pedro Almindez.

[6] Cortes was at Mexico when he wrote this.

tion, and garrison; I ordered some pieces of cannon to be placed in the Atarazanas, and the brigantines to be made ready, and I appointed an alcayde or military governor for the defence of the city, as well as for any other offensive operation that might be required. All this being accomplished, I set out with the said purpose from this city of Tenuxtitlan, and having reached Espiritu Santo, which is a town in the province of Coazacoalco,[1] distant one hundred and ten leagues from this city, whilst engaged in settling the internal affairs of the community, I dispatched messengers to Tabasco and Xiculango, informing the lords of those provinces of my intended journey, and ordering them to come and meet me, or send persons to whom I might communicate my instructions, adding that their deputies were to be men of probity and understanding, and such as could repeat to them faithfully the substance of my words. They did exactly as I told them; they received my messengers with due honour; and they sent me seven or eight worthy men duly authorised, as they are in the habit of doing on such occasions. Having inquired of these men the news of the land, I was told that on the sea-coast, beyond the region called Yucatan, towards the bay of the Asuncion,[2] there were certain Spaniards who did them much harm, since, besides burning their villages and slaying their people—in consequence of which many places were deserted, and the

[1] Now called Huazacoalco.

[2] This appears to be the same called Ascension in the maps; but in the Roman Catholic calendar Ascension and Asuncion are two different things, the former being only applicable to Jesus, the other to Mary. Ascension bay is really on the coast of Yucatan; yet the Spaniards who had gone under Gil Gonzalez Davila were not settled there, but about sixty leagues lower down, on the shores of the gulf called Amatico. Lorenzana, in his *History of New Spain*, p. 304, describes the bay of La Ascension as being formed by the waters of the Rio Grande, opposite the coast of the ancient province of Vera Paz, then united to the dioceses of Guatemala. In 1524 one of Cortes' pilots, named Diego Hurtado, visited it, whilst in search of a passage leading to the South Sea.

inhabitants had fled to the mountains—they had been the cause of the total disappearance of trade, formerly very flourishing, on that coast. Some of them, who had been in those parts, described to me most of the villages of the coast, as far as the place of residence of Pedrarias Davila, who now governs those regions in your Majesty's name; and drew on a cloth a figure of the whole land, whereby I calculated that I could very well go over the greater part of it, and in particular over that portion of the country which was pointed out to me as the abode of the said Spaniards.

Thus instructed about the road which I was to take in order to carry out my plans, and bring the natives of the land to the knowledge of our holy Catholic faith, and your Majesty's service—certain as I was that on so long a journey I would have to traverse many different provinces, and meet people of various races—being also curious to know whether the Spaniards mentioned to me were the same that I had sent under the captains Christoval de Olid, Pedro de Alvarado, or Francisco de las Casas, I considered it useful to your Majesty's service to go thither in person, inasmuch as my journey being through regions and provinces hitherto unexplored, I would have ample opportunity of doing service to your Majesty, and putting the said countries by peaceful means under the imperial rule, as has since been done.

Having, therefore, fixed on this idea, and regardless of the dangers and costly expense of such a journey, which some of my people did not fail to represent to me, I resolved to follow that route, as it was my first intention when I left this city. But before my arrival at the town of Espiritu Santo, at two or three places along the road, I received letters from this great city of Tenuxtitlan, in which the lieutenants I had appointed informed me how the treasurer and accounting-master had quarrelled, and how there was no longer between them that conformity of ideas which was so necessary for the proper discharge of their respective offices, and the trusts given to them in your Majesty's name. The same complaints were made in other letters written by private individuals to the officials who were then with me. I thereupon took those measures which I deemed most proper to arrest the evil, writing forthwith to both parties letters, wherein I reproached severely their conduct, and warned them that, unless they made their peace, and acted in conformity with each other, I would adopt measures unpleasant to either, and put the whole affair under the cognisance of your Majesty.

After this, during my stay in the said town of Espiritu Santo, and whilst I was preparing to set out on my journey, fresh letters came from the said lieutenants and from other persons, purporting how the enmity and bad passions of the treasurer and accounting-master still lasted, and had even increased so far that upon one occasion, as the two officials were sitting with others in council, they had actually drawn their swords one against another, the scandal and noise thus raised among the Spaniards being so great that they took up arms and divided into two factions. Even the natives of the city had been on the point of arming themselves, believing that noise and movement to be intended against them.

Seeing, therefore, that neither my remonstrances nor my threats were sufficient to put down the evil, and that I could not go thither myself and attend to its remedy unless I desisted altogether from my expedition, I determined upon sending to that city the factor and veedor, who, as I have already stated, were with me at the time; and I gave them full powers, equal to those of the two contending parties, to inquire into the causes of the dispute, to investigate which of them was wrong, and to compel them to keep their peace. In case of resistance, I furnished them with other secret powers and instructions to suspend them both in their offices, and take into their own hands the government of the city, conjointly with the licenciate Alonso de Zuazo, after punishing the guilty parties accordingly. The said factor Gonzalo de Salazar, and Peralmindez Chirino, the veedor, departed to fulfil their commission, and I remained with my mind very much at ease under the conviction that they would succeed in quieting the rival passions.

This being done, I took muster of the forces I had with me to prosecute my journey, and found them to consist of ninety-three horse, besides crossbowmen and arquebusiers, and thirty and odd foot, making in all a total of 230 men.[1] I next attended to the provender. There was then at anchor in the port of the said town of Espiritu Santo a large caravel, which had been sent to me from the town of Medellin, loaded with provisions. This I again filled with the stores I had brought with me; and, putting into it four pieces of artillery, as well as crossbows, muskets and other ammunition, directed the crew to sail for the island of Tabasco, and wait there for my commands. I also wrote to a servant of mine, who resides at the said town of Medellin, to load with provisions two other caravels and a large boat, then in the port, and send them to me. To Rodrigo de Paz, whom I left in charge of my house and property in this city

[1] The Vienna copy has "*y hallé noventa y tres de caballo, que entre todos habia ciento y cincuenta caballos, y treinta y tantos peones*, thus involving an error and a contradiction. Rodrigo de Albornoz, in a letter dated from Mexico the 15th of December, 1525, states the number to have been one hundred and twenty horse, twenty men armed with *escopetas* or short muskets, and as many crossbowmen and foot soldiers; whilst Bernal Diaz, who, as is well known, accompanied the expedition, says: "We were in all, between Guaçacualcan and Mexican settlers, two hundred and fifty soldiers, one hundred and thirty of them mounted, the remainder *escopeteros* (musketeers) and crossbowmen, without counting in that number a great many soldiers newly arrived from Castile." His own personal retinue consisted of several pages, young men of good family, and among them Montejo, the future conqueror of Yucatan, a butler and steward, several musicians, dancers, jugglers and buffoons; but all considered, the Spanish force under Cortes could not have much exceeded three hundred men, exclusive of the Mexican Indians.

of Tenuxtitlan, I gave instructions to remit to Medellin five or six thousand ounces of gold, to pay for the said provisions, and I even wrote to the treasurer begging him to advance me that money, as I had none left in the hands of the aforesaid agent. All this was done according to my wishes : the caravels came as far as the river of Tabasco, laden with provisions, though they proved to be of little use, because my route being far inland, neither the caravels, laden as they were, could go further up the river, nor could I send for them, owing to certain large morasses that lay between.

This matter of the provender to be dispatched by sea being thus settled, I began my journey, and marched along the coast until I reached a province called Çupilco,[1] about thirty-five leagues distant from the town of Espiritu Santo. On my road there, besides several morasses and water-streams, over all of which temporary bridges were thrown, I had to cross three very large rivers, one of them near a village called Túmalon, about nine leagues off the town of Espiritu Santo, the other at Agualulco, nine leagues farther on. These two were passed in canoes, the horses being led by the hand, and swimming across. The third river was so large and wide that it would have been impossible for the horses to swim across, and therefore I was obliged to look out for a more convenient spot up the stream, where I had a wooden bridge made for their passage and that of the men. It was a wonderful thing to behold, for the river measured at that spot nine hundred and thirty-four spans in width.

This province of Çupilco abounds in the fruit called cacao, and in other land produce. It has likewise good fisheries, and ten or twelve large villages, without counting the small ones. The land is low, and consequently full of morasses, so much so that in winter-time it is impossible to

---

[1] Thus, in the Vienna MS.; other copies read Zupilco, and even Cuplisco. Bernal Diaz (fol. 196) writes Coplisco. It is no doubt the Tupilcos of the maps.

go about except in canoes. I traversed it in dry weather; and yet, from the time I entered these morasses until I went out of them—a distance of about twenty leagues—I had to construct no less than fifty bridges for the passage of men and horses. The inhabitants are quiet and peaceful, though rather timid and shy, owing to the scanty communications they have hitherto had with Spaniards. Through my arrival among them, they became more secure and confident, serving with entire good will, not only me and the Spaniards I brought with me, but also those in whose hands I left them[1] on my departure.

From this province of Çupilco I was to proceed, according to the sketch or map given to me by the people of Tabasco and Xiculango, to another province called Çagoatan;[2] but as the natives of those regions only travel by water, none could shew me the land route, though they pointed out with their fingers that part of the map where the said province was supposed to be. I was therefore obliged to send in that direction some of my Spaniards and Indians to look out for a road, and, when found, to make it practicable for the rest of us, as our way was forcibly through very high mountains. It, however, pleased God Almighty that such a road was found, though hard and difficult in the extreme, not only on account of the said mountain-ridge to be traversed, but also of the many perilous marshes, over all of which, or the greater part, we had to throw bridges. After this it became necessary to cross a very large river, called Queçalapa, one of the tributaries of the Tabasco.

---

[1] According to the practice introduced by the conquerors and sanctioned by the court, the Indians were distributed as vassals among the Spaniards, a certain number of them being *encomendados*, *i.e.*, entrusted or given in charge to each of the conquerors or settlers, according to their respective rank, position or services. The community of Indians thus allotted to a Spaniard was known by the name of *encomienda*; and the lord himself, for such he became over his Indian vassals, was called *encomendero*, that is, owner of an *encomienda*.

[2] Sometimes written Zagoatan.

To complete my arrangements, I dispatched towards the
lords of Tabasco and Cunuapá two of my Spaniards, begging
them to send up the Tabasco river from fifteen to twenty of
their canoes, that might bring provisions from the huge
caravel stationed there, and help me in the crossing of the
river. I requested them, moreover, to take the said provisions as far as a principal town called Çagoatan, situated up
the river, and, as it afterwards appeared, distant about
twelve leagues from the spot where I crossed. They did as
I desired them to do, all my orders being very punctually
executed.

Having thus found the road to the river Zalapa,[1] which,
as stated, we had necessarily to cross, I set out from the last
village in the province of Çupilco, called Anaxuxuan, and
passed that first night in a deserted spot surrounded by
lakoons. Early the next day we arrived on the banks of the
river, but found no canoes there for the passage of the men,
those which I had asked from the lords of Tabasco not having yet reached their destination. I learned, moreover, that
the pioneers whom I had sent forwards were cutting their
way up the river from the other side, because, having been informed that it passed through the most important town in all
the province of Çagoatan, they naturally followed up its
course not to be mistaken. One of them, in order to arrive
sooner at the said town, had gone by water in a canoe, and
on his arrival had found the natives in a state of great ex-
citement and fear. He spoke to them through an interpreter
he had with him; and having succeeded in quieting their
minds a little, he sent back his canoe down the river, with
some Indians, to inform me how he had made his entrance
into the town, and had been well received by the natives.
That he was coming down himself with a number of Indians,
opening the road by which I was to travel until he should

[1] The same river called elsewhere Quezalapa, and which is also written
by the copyist sometimes Gueçalapa, others Zuezalapa.

meet with the pioneers, who were working on this other side. This intelligence gave me great delight, not only because it announced the peaceable inclinations of those people, but because it gave me the certitude of a road, when I considered it as rather doubtful, or at least as difficult and dangerous.

With the canoe which brought those Indians, and with some rafters which I ordered to be constructed out of large pieces of timber, I managed to send all the heavy luggage on the other side of the river, which in that place is of very considerable width. Whilst engaged in the crossing, the Spaniards, whom I had sent to Tabasco, arrived with twenty canoes laden with provisions out of the great caravel which I had sent there from Coazacoalco.[1] From these people I learned that the two other great caravels and the boat had not yet arrived in the river, having remained behind at Coazacoalco; but that they were expected soon. In the said canoes came also no less than two hundred Indians from the provinces of Tabasco and Cunuapá,[2] with whose help the crossing of the river was effected, without any other accident but the drowning of a negro slave and the loss of two loads of iron tools, whereof we afterwards stood in some need. That night I slept on the other side of the river with all my people, and on the next day began to follow the track of the pioneers, who were opening the road, my only guide being the banks of the river itself. In this manner we marched about six leagues, and arrived under a very heavy rain at a mountain where we slept. During the night, the Spaniard who had gone up the river to Çagoatan came back with about seventy Indians, all natives

---

[1] The Vienna copy Zoazala, which is evidently a mistake. It was at the port of Espiritu Santo, in the province of Cozacoalco, that Cortes dispatched to Tabasco the vessel that came from Medellin. *Vide supra*, p. 6.

[2] No doubt the same which Bernal Diaz (fol. 196) calls Iquinuapá.

of that place, and informed me how he had succeeded in opening a road on the other side, but that if I chose to take it, it was necessary for me to retrace my steps for a distance of two leagues. I did so, but I gave orders at the same time that the pioneers—who were in advance cutting their way on the bank of the river, and were already three leagues off the place where I had passed the night—should go on with their work. They had scarcely advanced one league and a half, when they fell in with the outskirts of the town, and by this means two roads were opened where there was none before.

I followed the one opened by the natives, and though it proved rather a hard one, on account of the rain that fell by torrents, and of the many morasses we had to cross, I yet managed to arrive on that same day at one of the suburbs of the said town, which, though the smallest of all, contained, nevertheless, upwards of two hundred houses. We could not go to the others, because they were separated by rivers that ran betwixt, and which could only be crossed by swimming. All of them, however, were deserted, and, moreover, we found on our arrival that all the Indians who had accompanied the Spaniard, had also taken flight, notwithstanding I spoke to them in mild terms and treated them well, distributing among them some of the trifles I had with me, and thanking them for the pains they had taken in opening the said road. I had told them that my coming to those parts was by the command of your Majesty, and for no other purpose than to teach them how to believe in and worship an only God, creator and maker of all things, and acknowledge your Majesty as supreme lord of the land. Many other like things I had told them which are customary on such occasions, and yet, as I said before, the inhabitants had fled to a man. I waited three or four days, thinking they had only left through fear, and that they might come back to speak to me; but not one made his appearance.

Upon which, in order to communicate with them, and bring them by peaceable means to your Majesty's service, as well as ascertain from them which way the road lay through a country quite unexplored, full of large rivers and deep marshes, and which seemed never to have been trod by human foot—the natives themselves never travelling except by water—I determined, the better to attain the two objects above stated, to send two companies of Spaniards, and some of the natives of this city of Tenuxtitlan and its adjoining territory who were with me, with orders to seize upon and bring to me any Indians that might be found in the said province.

By means, therefore, of those canoes that had come up the river from Tabasco, and of others that we procured belonging to the said town, my men managed to navigate most of those rivers and morasses, all marching through land being deemed impracticable; but they could only discover two Indians and some women, of whom I took every pains to ascertain whither the people of their town and the lord of the land had fled. The only answer I could obtain from them was that the people of the country had all dispersed over the mountains, or were hiding in the rivers and swamps of the vicinity. Having, moreover, inquired from them the road to the province of Chilapan—which, according to the sketch I had with me, lay next on my route—they never would tell me, alleging that their only mode of travelling was by rivers and marshes in their canoes, never by land; that they knew how to go thither by water, and not otherwise. They did, however, point out to me a chain of mountains, which might be about ten leagues off, saying that in its neighbourhood stood the principal town of the province of Chilapan, on the banks of a large river, which, uniting lower down its waters to those of the Cagoatan, became afterwards a tributary of the Tabasco. That up that river (the Cagoatan) there was another village, called Acumba;

but that they were unable to shew me the way thither by land.

At this town of Çagoatan we remained twenty days, incessantly occupied in finding out some road that might take us onwards; but the country around us was so full of morasses and lakoons, that we could not stir out of the place, and all our efforts proved in vain. Yet we were soon placed in such a state of jeopardy, through the exhaustion of our provisions, that we made up our minds to risk our lives in the attempt. Accordingly, having previously commended our souls to God our Creator, we threw a bridge over a morass, three hundred paces in length; and on this bridge, which was formed by many large pieces of timber, measuring thirty five or forty feet in length, crossed by others of similar dimensions, we passed the said morass, setting out immediately in search of that chain of mountains near to which stood, as we were told, the town of Chilapan. In the meanwhile, I sent by another route a troop of horsemen and certain archers in the direction of the other village, called Acumba, and they were fortunate enough to find it that very day. Having swam through a river, or crossed it in two canoes which they found on its bank, they came suddenly upon the village, whose inhabitants took to flight. My men found inside plenty of provision, two Indians and some women, with whom they came to meet me. I slept that night in the fields.

On the next day God permitted that we should come to a country more open and dry, and less covered with swamps, so that, guided by the Indians taken at Acumba,[1] we arrived the day after, at a very late hour, at the town of Chilapan,

---

[1] The name of this place is differently written in the copies that I have examined: some have Attumba, others Acumba. That of the Royal Academy, Acumbra; whilst the Vienna one, which appears the most ancient, reads distinctly Ocumba. There are not wanting writers who identify it with Cicimbra.

which we found completely burnt down, and its inhabitants all gone.

This town of Chilapan is beautifully situated, and very large. It is surrounded by plantations of trees, bearing the usual fruits of the land: the fields were filled with maize or Indian corn, which, though not yet in all its maturity, was of great help to us in our necessity.

I remained ten days at Chilapan, laying in provisions for the journey, and ordering certain excursions to be made in the neighbourhood, with a view to secure, if possible, some natives from whom I might learn the road; but with the exception of two, who were at first found hiding in the village, all our search was in vain. From these, however, I ascertained upon inquiry the road to Tepetitan,[1] otherwise called Tamacastepeque; and, although they hardly knew their way thither, we were lucky enough, sometimes through their leading, and at others by our own device, to reach that place on the second day. We had to cross a very large river, called Chilapan, wherefrom the aforesaid town takes its name; which was done with great difficulty, owing to the depth of the waters and the rapidity of the current: we used rafts, there being no canoes at the place; and we lost a negro, who was drowned, and much luggage belonging to my Spaniards.

After this river, which we crossed at a place distant one league and a half from the said village of Chilapan, we had to pass, before reaching Tepetitan, several extensive and deep swamps or morasses, in all of which except one the horses sank deep to their knees, and sometimes to their ears. Between Chilapan and Tepetitan, a distance of six or seven leagues, the ground was covered with similar swamps; one, in particular, we found so dangerous that, although a bridge

[1] Sometimes written Tepetiçan or Tepetizan, which comes to the same, Spaniards of this time using indifferently the letters ç and z to express analogous sounds.

was thrown over it, yet two or three Spaniards were very near being drowned.

After two days of very fatiguing march we reached the said village of Tepetitan, which we found also burnt down and deserted, our troubles and anxiety being thereby much increased. We found inside some fruits of the land, and in the neighbourhood fields of maize still unripe, though taller than that of Chilapan. We also discovered, under some of the burnt houses, granaries with small quantities of dried [Indian] corn, which were of great help in the extremity to which we had been reduced.

At this village of Tepetitan, which stands at the foot of a chain of mountains, I stayed six full days, causing inroads to be made in search of natives who might be persuaded to return peaceably to their dwellings, and point out to us the road to follow next. My Spaniards could only find one man and some women, from whom I learned that the chief and inhabitants of the town had been induced by the people of Çagoatan to set fire to their village and fly to the mountains. The Indian did not know the way to Iztapan, the next place on my map, there being, as he said, no road to it by land; but he undertook to guide me towards the spot where he knew it to stand.

With this Indian as a guide, I sent thirty of my Spaniards on horseback, and thirty more on foot, with instructions to find out the village of Iztapan, and once in it to write to me a description of the road which I was to follow, determined as I was not to move from the place where I had encamped until I heard from them. They started on their expedition; but at the end of two days, having received no letters, nor otherwise heard from them—seeing, moreover, the extreme want to which we were reduced, I decided to follow them without a guide, and with no other indication of the road they had taken than the impression of their footsteps in the awfully miry swamps with which the country is covered; for

I can assure your Majesty that even on the top of the hills our horses, led as they were by hand, and without their riders, sank to their girths in the mire.

In this manner I marched for two consecutive days without receiving any tidings of the people I had sent forward to Iztapan, and therefore greatly puzzled as to what I was to do next; for to go back was impossible, and to proceed on my march without having a certainty of the road, seemed to me equally dangerous. In this perplexity, God, who in our greatest afflictions comes often to our help, was pleased to permit that, whilst we were encamped in great sadness and tribulation, thinking that we were all doomed to perish of hunger, two Indians should arrive bearing letters from those Spaniards whom I had sent onwards. They informed me that on their arrival at the village of Iztapan, they found that the natives had sent all their women and property across a large river, which ran close to the place, and that the village itself was full of natives thinking that they (the Spaniards) would not be able to pass a great morass close to it. However, when they saw my men swimming across it on their horses, they were very much frightened, and began to set fire to their village. In this they were prevented by my men, who hastened to put it out, seeing which, all the inhabitants took to their heels and ran to the bank of the river, which they crossed, either in numerous canoes they had there, or by swimming; the haste and confusion occasioned by it being so great, that many of them were drowned. My Spaniards, nevertheless, had succeeded in securing seven or eight, among whom there was one who seemed to be a chief. The letter further added that they were anxiously expecting my arrival.

I cannot describe to your Majesty the joy this unexpected news caused among my men; for at the time it came they were almost in a state of despair, as I said before. Early on the next day I followed the track, being also guided by

the Indians who had brought the letter, and in this manner
arrived at Iztapan late in the evening. I there found the
Spaniards in a high state of glee, owing to their having
discovered, besides many maize plantations—though the grain
had not yet reached its maturity—great abundance of *yuca*
and *agi*,[1] two plants which constitute the principal food of
the people of the Islands,[2] and make a tolerably good meal.

Immediately upon my arrival at Iztapan, I sent for the
natives who had been taken prisoners, and asked them,
through an interpreter, what could be the reason of their
thus setting fire to their houses and deserting their village,
when I intended them no harm, but on the contrary had
always given those who remained part of what I had with
me. Their answer was that the lord of Çagoatan had
arrived among them in a canoe, and had frightened them
very much, making them set their village on fire and desert
it. I then summoned the chief man to my presence, as well
as the Indians of both sexes taken at Çagoatan, Chilapan,
and Tepetitan, and explained to him how the lord of Çagoatan
was a bad man, who had deceived them; and that, in order
to test the truth of my words, he had only to interrogate
those Indians now before him, and ask them whether I or
any of my people had ever done them any injury. He did
ask them; and having heard from their own mouths how
kindly I had behaved towards them, they all began to cry,
saying how much they had been deceived, and shewing
their sorrow for what they had done. I then, in order to
give them more security and confidence, granted permission
to all the Indians who had come with me from the other
villages to return to their homes, giving them some trifles,

[1] *Aji*, sometimes written *agi*, is the red Indian dwarf pepper of which
the Mexicans of the present day still make use for their meals. As to
the *yuca*, it is the plant generally known as Adam's needle, the root of
which is farinaceous.

[2] By "las Islas," the islands, the Spaniards of this day meant Cuba,
Puerto Rico, Santo Domingo, and other western islands.

as well as certain letters of mine for each village, which
I said they were to keep carefully by them, and shew to
any Spaniards who chanced to pass by, in order not to be
in the least molested. I likewise recommended them to say
to their chiefs, as coming from me, what mischief they had
done in setting fire to their villages and deserting their
homes; that they were not to do it again, but on the
contrary to remain in their respective dwellings, whenever
Spaniards came to their villages, under the security that no
harm or injury would be inflicted upon them.

When the people of Iztapan heard this, they went away
greatly satisfied and happy, which was the means of inspiring security to the inhabitants of other villages in the
neighbourhood. After this, I addressed myself to that
Indian who seemed to be a chief among them, and told him
to mind how I did no harm to any one about me; neither
had I come to those parts for the purpose of offending
them, but on the contrary, to teach them many things well
suited for the security of their persons, and the welfare and
salvation of their souls. That I therefore begged he would
send two or three of those Indians who were in his company,
to whom I would add an equal number from among the
natives of Tenuxtitan, to deliver a message from me to the
lord of Iztapan, and persuade him to come back to his
village without fear, and under the certainty that no harm
would be done to him or his people, but on the contrary he
would be greatly benefited by his return. The Indian
having shewn his readiness to execute my message, started
immediately on his errand, accompanied by some Mexicans.
On the morning of the next day he came back, bringing
with him the lord of Iztapan, and about forty natives of
that place, who had abandoned the place on the arrival of
my men. He assured me that if he set his village on fire
and fled, he did it at the instigation of the said lord of
Çagoatan, who had come in those parts telling him not to

wait for the arrival of the Spaniards, who would most
certainly put him and his people to death. But now that he
learned from his own people how much he had been deceived, and that the lord of Çagoatan had told him a lie, he
felt very sorry for what he had done, and accordingly
begged my pardon, shewing his readiness to do whatever
I might be pleased to order him. He, however, humbly
besought me to grant that some women, taken by the
Spaniards at the time they entered his village, should be
given back to him. I immediately complied with this
request, ordering that some twenty women, who were then
in the camp, and had been taken when the village was
entered, should be returned to him, at which he shewed
great satisfaction.

It happened, however, that a Spaniard saw one of the
Indians who had come with me from Tenuxtitlan eating
a piece of flesh taken from the body of another Indian,
whom he had killed on entering Iztapan. When the case
was reported to me, I had the Indian arrested, and there, in
the presence of the chief, had him burnt alive, for having
slain and afterwards eaten of his fellow-creature—an abomi-
nation which your Majesty, and I myself in your royal
name, have repeatedly deprecated, ordering the people of
those parts to abstain from it. I therefore made the lord
understand that if I punished that man with death, it was
because, in disobedience to your Majesty's commands, he
had slain and afterwards eaten of the flesh of his fellow-
creature. That my wish was that nobody should be hurt,
having been sent to those parts merely for the purpose of
protecting them and taking care of their property, as well as
shewing them the way of worshipping one only God, who
is in heaven, Creator and Maker of all things, by whose will
all living creatures are governed. In order to do this, they
were to relinquish all their idols and their abominable rites,
because they were nothing more than lies and deceptions of

the devil, who, being the sworn enemy of mankind, had devised those and other similar arts to ensure their perpetual damnation in the midst of horrible and everlasting tortures. That the devil was thus trying to lead them away from the knowledge of one only and true God, shutting them from the path of salvation, and preventing by all means in his power that they should partake of that glory and blessed happiness awaiting those who believe in God, in an abode of everlasting bliss, which the devil himself had lost owing to his disobedience and malice.

That another of the objects of my mission was to inform them how, by the will of divine Providence, your Majesty stood obeyed and respected throughout the world, and therefore that they were bound to place themselves under the imperial sway, and do whatever we, who are your Majesty's ministers in these parts, should command them to do. If they did as I told them, they were sure to be very well treated, and maintained in justice, and their persons and properties protected; if on the contrary, proceedings would be instituted against them, and they would be punished according to law. Many other things I told them to the same end, which I omit for brevity's sake.

Great was the joy shewn by the lord of Iztapan when he heard this discourse of mine. He immediately ordered some of the Indians who had come with him to go back and bring provisions, which they did. I gave him a few trifles of Spanish manufacture, which pleased him exceedingly; and he remained in my company as long as I stayed at Iztapan. After this, he ordered some of his men to open a road for me to a village called Tatahuitalpan,[1] five leagues up the river; and as there was in the way thither a very deep river, he caused a beautiful bridge to be made, over which we crossed, and had also some morasses of the very worst description arranged and filled for our passage. He

---

[1] Sometimes written Yatahuïtalpan.

likewise gave me three canoes, in which I sent as many Spaniards down the river to Tabasco—this being one of its principal tributaries—where the great caravels, as I said before, were waiting for my orders. They were to follow the coast till they came to a cape, called Yucatan, which they were to double, and then proceed to Assumption[1] Bay, where they would find me, or else receive instructions as to what they were to do next. I, moreover, gave orders to the three Spaniards who went down the river that, using their three canoes, and all those they could collect in the provinces of Tabasco and Xiculango, they should bring me as many provisions as they could by a great sheet of water[2] communicating with the province of Aculan, forty leagues distant from Iztapan, where I would wait for them.

The Spaniards being gone to their destination and the road completed, I begged the lord of Iztapan to give me three or four more canoes, and some of his people, under a chief, who might accompany six of my Spaniards up the river, and endeavour, as they went on, to quiet the natives and prevent their setting fire to their villages and deserting them. This he did with every appearance of good will, and my people, accompanied as they were by Indians from Iztapan, succeeded in appeasing the inhabitants of four or five villages up the river, as I will hereafter inform your Majesty.

Iztapan is a very fine town. It is situated on the bank of a very large river, and has many advantages which make it a fit abode for Spaniards. Pasture is excellent along the banks of the river: it has good arable land, and its territory is well peopled.

---

[1] It has already been observed elsewhere that this bay is now called in the maps Ascension Bay.

[2] The word used is *estero*, which in these times meant an arm of the sea, a piece of water, sweet or salt, far inland; sometimes, also, a creek or small port, a gulf.

Having spent eight days at Iztapan, and issued for the
maintenance of my people the orders specified in the above
paragraph, I set out for Tatahuitalpan, where I arrived the
same day, and found the village—which was a small one—
entirely burnt down and deserted.   I was the first to arrive
by land, because the canoes I had sent up the river found
the current so strong, and met with so many windings, that
they could not come up in time.   No sooner did they arrive,
than I sent them across the river in search of some natives
whom I could speak to, and induce, as I had the others
before them, to return peaceably to their dwellings.   About
half a league inland, my men met with some twenty Indians
inside a house or temple, where they had a number of idols
very finely arrayed.   Being brought into my presence,
they informed me that all their countrymen had deserted
the place through fear, but that as to themselves, they had
preferred remaining on the spot and dying next to their
idols.   Whilst I was conversing with them, some of our
Mexican Indians happened to pass by loaded with things
taken from those very idols ; which, being observed by the
people, they set up a cry, saying : " Our gods are dead."
Hearing this, I addressed myself to them, and told them to
consider what a vain and foolish thing their creed was, since
they placed their trust and confidence in rude idols which
had not even the power of protecting themselves, and could
not prevent their own ruin and destruction.   Their answer
was that their fathers had lived in that creed, and that until
they knew of a better one, they would persevere in it.   I
could not for the moment tell them on this subject more
than I had already said to the   'ple of Iztapan ; but
two Franciscan friars, who cam﹐ in﹐ .ny suite, conversed at
some length with them on matters of religion.

I requested some of these Indians to go in search of their
own countrymen, and bring them, as well as their chief,
back to the village.   The Iztapan chief whom I had with me at

the time also spoke to them, mentioning the good treatment he
and his people had experienced at our hands whilst in possession of their village. Upon which the Indians pointed
out one of themselves, saying "this is our lord"; and he
immediately dispatched two of them towards the people,
bidding them to return, which they never did.

Seeing that they refused to come back, I desired that
Indian who had declared himself to be their lord to shew me
the road to Çagoatespan,[1] a place up the river, through
which I had necessarily to pass if I was to follow the
indications of the map given to me by the people of Tabasco.
He answered that he knew not the way by land, but only
by water, which was their sole mode of travelling. He,
nevertheless, offered to do his best, and guide us through
those mountains, hoping he might find his way. I did not
accept his services, but told him and his people to point out
to me the spot where the village stood, which they did.
I marked it down on the map, in the best manner I could,
and ordered the Spaniards who were in the canoes to take
along with them that Iztapan chief, and go up the river
until they should come to the said village of Çagoatespan.
Arrived there, they were to do their utmost to appease the
people of the said village, as well as those of another one
called Ozumazintlan,[2] which they must necessarily meet on
their way. If I arrived first, I would wait for them; if on
the contrary, they were to wait for me.

This matter being settled and the Spaniards gone on their
expedition, I took the land road, preceded by those guides.
No sooner had we left the village of Tatahuitalpan than we
came to a great morass, upwards of half a league in length,
which we managed to pass, the Indians, our friends, having

---

[1] The Vienna copy has Zaguatapan; we read in others Siguateçpan: it is
perhaps the same place called Ciguatepecad by Bernal Diaz, fol. 198, vº.

[2] This name has been corrupted by the copyists into Cocuniazantan
and Coçuniazantlan.

helped us by laying on our path great quantity of grass and branches of trees. After this we came to a very deep lagoon, over which we were compelled to throw a bridge for the passage of the heavy luggage and of the horses' saddles, the horses themselves swimming across it led by the hand. Immediately after this we came to another deep lagoon, extending for more than one league, and occasionally intersected by swamps, where our horses sank always knee-deep, and sometimes as far as the girdles; but the ground at the bottom being rather harder than usual, we passed it without accident, and arrived at the foot of a mountain covered with thick wood. We cut our way through this as well as we could for two consecutive days, until our guides declared that they had lost all traces of the road, and could proceed no further. The mountain was so high, and the forest so thick and impenetrable, that we could only see the spot where we placed our feet, or, looking upwards, the blue sky over our heads; and the trees were so tall and so close to each other, that those who climbed up them to discover land could not see beyond a stone's throw.

As the Spaniards who had been sent forwards with the guides to cut a path through the mountain communicated to me this painful information, I gave immediate orders that they should remain where they were, whilst I proceeded thither on foot that I might judge by myself of the gravity of the case. Having found upon inspection that the report was but too true, I made the people go back to a small morass which we had passed the day before, and where, on account of the water in it, there was some grass for the horses to eat, for they had not tasted anything for forty-eight hours. There we remained all that night greatly tormented by hunger, which was further increased by the little hope we had of arriving at a place of habitation. In this emergency, and seeing my people more dead than alive, I asked for a marine compass, which I was in the habit of carrying always with

me, and which had often been of much use—though never
so much as on that occasion—and recollecting the spot
where the Indians had told me that the village stood, I found
by calculation that, by marching in a north-eastern direction,
we should come upon the village, or very near to it. I then
ordered those who went forwards cutting the road to take
that compass, and to guide themselves by it, which they did.
And thus it pleased our Lord that my calculations turned
out so true, that about the hour of vespers my men fell in
with some idol-houses in the centre of the village. On
hearing which the rest of my people felt so great a joy, that
they all ran in that direction, without heeding a large
swamp that stood in their way, and in which many horses
sank so deep that they could not be extricated from it until
the next day, God, however, permitting that we should not
lose one of them. Those who were in the rear with me
crossed the swamp in another direction, and were fortunate
enough to reach the place without accident, although with
considerable trouble and difficulty.

Çagoatespan was entirely burnt down, even to the mosques[1]
and idol-houses. We found nobody in the town, as it was
completely deserted, and therefore could not obtain news of
the canoes I had sent up the river. There was plenty of
maize riper than that of other places, yuca and peppers,
besides good pasture for our horses, the banks of the river,
which seemed very fertile, being covered with very fine
grass. Thus refreshed, we began to forget some of our
past troubles, although I, in particular, felt great anxiety at
not hearing news of the canoes I had sent up the river.
I was in this village looking about me, and examining the
neighbouring districts, when I saw an arrow planted in the

[1] The Spanish *mezquita*, from the Arabic *mesjid*, means a mosque, a
place of worship for Mahometans; but the writers of the fifteenth
century used that word indiscriminately to designate any spot for
pagan worship.

earth, which to me was a proof of the canoes having passed
that spot, for all the men I sent in them were archers; but
this very circumstance made me suspect that they might have
since come to blows with the people of the village, and been
slain in the affray, since they did not make their appearance.
In order to ascertain, if possible, the truth, I put some of
my people in certain small canoes that were there found,
and sent them across the river to explore. They soon met
with a great number of Indians, and saw many cultivated
fields, and, proceeding on their errand, came upon a large
lake, where, partly in canoes and partly in certain small
islands, all the people of the village had congregated;
though, at sight of the Spaniards, instead of running away,
as usual, they came up to meet them with great glee, and said
things which my people could not understand. They, however, brought to my presence some thirty or forty of them,
whom I addressed through an interpreter, putting the usual
questions to them. Their answer was that they had been
induced by the lord of Çagoatan to set fire to their village
and take shelter in those lakes where they now were, all
this being done through fear of us. That after this they
had been visited by some of my men coming there in boats,
as well as by natives of Iztapan, from whom they had
learned the good treatment I gave to all Indians, whereby
their fears had subsided. That my Spaniards had been
there two days waiting for me, but seeing I did not come,
they had gone up the river to another village, called Petenecte,
accompanied by a brother of their chief and some people in
four canoes, to help them in case of need against the inhabitants of that place; that they had besides given them
plenty of provisions and everything else they could want.

This news gave me great satisfaction; and as the bearers
had come to me of their own accord, I had no difficulty in
believing them. I, however, begged they would send for
one of their canoes, and dispatch it with a crew in search of

those Spaniards of mine who had gone up the river to Petenecte. They were to take them a letter of mine with orders not to go any further and come back to me. This they did in a very short time; for on the evening of next day, at the hour of vespers, my Spaniards made their appearance, followed by the Indians who had gone in search of them, as well as by four canoes laden with provisions and manned by Indians belonging to the village whence they came.

Having asked the said Spaniards to tell me their adventures up the river from the time they left me at Tatahuitalpan, their report was as follows: When they arrived at Ozumazintlan,[1] the village immediately above this, they found the place completely destroyed by fire, and the inhabitants very much frightened; but upon the arrival of the people of Iztapan, who accompanied them, some of the fugitives had been persuaded to return to their homes, their fears had subsided, and they had given the Spaniards food and everything else they asked for. After this they had gone to Çagoatespan, which they also found deserted, and the inhabitants gone to the opposite side of the river; but on the people of Iztapan coming up and speaking to them, they came back to their village and received the Spaniards very well, giving them in abundance of everything they could want. There they had waited two days for me, but seeing that I did not come, and believing that I was gone to some place further up the river, they had determined to go on to Petenecte,[2] which is six leagues beyond Çagoatespan, taking with them as guides the people of that village and a brother of their chief. They found Petenecte deserted, though not burnt down, and the inhabitants on the opposite bank of the river; but the people of Iztapan and those of

[1] The Vienna copy Uzumazintlan, in others Imacintlan; but as there can be no doubt that it is the same village mentioned in p. 23, I have adopted that reading.

[2] Sometimes written Penecte, with the omission of one syllable.

Çagoatespan had spoken to them, and inspired them with
confidence, and induced them to come and see me; and they
were actually coming down in four canoes, bringing maize,
honey, cocao, and a small quantity of gold. They had sent
messengers to three more villages up the river, named
Coazacoalco,[1] Caltencingo and Teutitan, and they believed
that on the next day they would come to see me. So they
did; for at the appointed hour we saw coming down the
river seven or eight canoes filled with people from those
three villages, who brought pounded maize, and gold in
small quantities. I spoke to them for some time, and tried
to make them understand how they were to believe in God,
and serve your Majesty. Every one of them promised then
and there to become your Majesty's vassal, to obey the
imperial commands, and do at any time whatever he might be
desired to do. In particular, the natives of that village
called Çagoatespan brought before me some of their idols,
and there, in my presence, broke them into pieces, and
having lighted a fire, threw them into it. After this the
principal chief of the place, who had not yet shown himself,
came and brought me some gold; and I gave every one of
them some of the trifles I had with me, whereupon they
were very much pleased, and felt very secure.

Having asked them the road to Aculan, there was some
difference of opinion among them; some, among whom were
the people of Çagoatespan, pretended that my way lay
through the villages up the river, and that they had pur-
posely caused six leagues of road to be opened up in that
direction, and ordered a bridge to be thrown over a certain
river which we should have to pass. Others maintained

---

[1] The names of these places, which it will be a vain task to look for
in the maps, are variously written in some of the MSS. Instead of
Coazacoalco, we have *Coalzasestal;* instead of Caltencingo, *Taltenango*
and *Caltancingo:* Teutitan is written *Tautitan, Testitan,* and even
Tabsenango. Coazacoalco must be a different place from that which was
the residence of Bernal Diaz. See p. 10.

that this route, besides being a very bad one, was by far the
longest, and that my best and shortest road to Acalan[1] was
to cross the river at the place where we were, for on the
other side we would find a small track which was very much
frequented and used by pedlars, and led straight to that
village. Finally, after much disputing, it was settled between
them that this last was the better road to take.

I had, on my first arrival at Çagoatespan, dispatched in
the direction of Aculan one of my Spaniards, accompanied
by several natives of the place, with instructions to inform
the people of that province of my intended visit, and
endeavour to appease them and calm their fears. My
messenger was likewise to ascertain whether those of my
people who had been entrusted with the bringing provisions
from the brigantines were arrived at their destination or
not. I now sent in that same direction four more Spaniards,
attended by guides selected from among the natives, and
who professed to know their way thither, in order that they
might report about it, and tell me whether the road was
practicable or not; they would find me at Çagoatespan,
where I was to wait for their answer.

But soon after the departure of the four Spaniards sent to
Aculan I changed my mind; and although I had promised
to remain at Çagoatespan until I should have their report,
I nevertheless considered myself bound to prosecute my
march. The reason was this: I was afraid that, by remaining there any length of time, the provisions I had made for
the journey would be exhausted, for I was told that we
should have to march five or six days without meeting a
single living soul.

I began, therefore, to pass the river in canoes, an operation
which, owing to its width and to the strength of the current,
could not be effected without some difficulty and danger.
One horse was drowned, and some packages belonging to

[1] Sometimes written Acalan.

my Spaniards were also lost.   Having, however, crossed the
river, I sent forward a troop of pioneers to open the road
in front, whilst I, with the rest of the men, followed in the
rear.   In this way, after traversing for three consecutive
days a mountainous district covered with thick wood, we
came by a very narrow path to a large lagoon, measuring
upwards of five hundred paces in width, and for the passage
of which we tried in vain to find a place: it could never be
found, neither up nor down, and our guides ended by
declaring that unless we marched for twenty consecutive
days in the direction of the mountains we should never be
able to turn that lagoon.

I cannot well describe what were my disappointment and
dismay on the receipt of such intelligence, for crossing that
deep lagoon seemed a matter of utter impossibility, on
account of its great width and of our not having boats.
Even if we had had them for the men and heavy luggage,
the horses would have found, in going in and out of it, most
awful morasses, sprinkled with roots and stems of trees, and
so shaped that, unless the beasts could fly over them, it was
quite out of the question to attempt the crossing.   Retracing
our steps was equivalent to certain death, not only on
account of the bad roads we had to go over, and the heavy
rains that had lately fallen, but because we would find no
food of any sort.   It was, moreover, evident that the rivers
had swollen since and carried away the bridges constructed
by us; to make these again was entirely out of the question,
for my people were exhausted by fatigue.   It was also
probable that we should find no provisions on the road, having
already eaten the little there was, and our numbers being
so considerable, for besides the Spaniards and their horses,
I was then followed by upwards of three thousand natives.

I have already stated above the difficulties that stood in
the way of our going on; the danger of retracing our steps
was equally great; so that no man's intelligence, however

powerful, could find means to extricate us from our position, if God, who is the true remedy and help in all afflictions, had not aided us. For when I was almost reduced to despair, I accidentally found a small canoe that had served for the passage of those Spaniards sent by me to inspect the road. I immediately took possession of it, and set about having the lagoon sounded, so as to ascertain the depth of its waters, which I found to be of at least four fathoms all the way. I then had some spears tied together and sunk into the water, to see the quality of the soil, and it was found that besides the said depth of four fathoms, there were at least two more of mud and mire at the bottom. There was, therefore, no other alternative left us save the construction of a bridge, however difficult the undertaking might prove, owing to the depth of the waters. I immediately set about distributing among the people the work to be done and the timber to cut. The beams or posts were to be from nine to ten fathoms in length, owing to the portion that was to remain above water. I gave orders that each Indian chief of those who followed our camp should, in proportion to the number of men he had under his orders, cut down and bring to the spot a certain number of trees of the required length, whilst I and my Spaniards, some of us on rafts and some in that canoe and in two more that were found afterwards, began to plant the posts in the bed of the river. But the work was so fatiguing, and so difficult at the same time, that all my men despaired of its ever being finished. Some even went so far as to privately express their opinion that it was far preferable to return now, than tarry until the men should be completely exhausted by fatigue and hunger; for the bridge could never be made fit for passage, and therefore, sooner or later, we should be compelled to abandon the undertaking and retrace our steps.

This opinion gained so much ground among my Spaniards, that they almost dared to utter it in my presence; upon

which, seeing them so disheartened—and I confess they
had good reasons to be so, the work I had undertaken
being of such a nature that we could hardly expect to see it
completed—knowing that we were without provisions, and
that for some days our only food had been the roots of
certain plants, I decided that they should no longer work at
the bridge, intending to make it exclusively with the help
of the Indians. I immediately sent for the chiefs of these,
and having explained to them what our situation was, I
told them that we must cross that river or perish in the
attempt. That I begged, therefore, they would unite their
efforts, and encourage their men to the construction of a
solid bridge, for the river once crossed, we would soon
come to a province called Aculan, where there was abundance of food, and where we might repose ourselves. That
besides the provisions of every kind to be had in that
country, they well knew how I had ordered that some
of that stored in the ships should be conveyed thither
in boats, so that upon our arrival we could not fail
to be provided with every necessary of life. Besides which,
I solemnly promised to them that upon our return to this
great city of Tenuxtitlan, whereof most of them were natives,
they would be most munificently rewarded by me in your
Majesty's name. They agreed to work at it *viribus et posse*,
and began at once to divide the task between them, and
I must say that they worked so hard, and with such good
will, that in less than four days they constructed a fine
bridge, over which the whole of the men and horses passed.
So solidly built it was, that I have no doubt it will stand
for upwards of ten years without breaking—unless it is
burnt down—being formed by upwards of one thousand
beams, the smallest of which was as thick round as a man's
body, and measured nine or ten fathoms in length, without
counting a great quantity of lighter timber that was used as
planks. And I can assure your Majesty that I do not

believe there is a man in existence capable of explaining in
a satisfactory manner the dexterity which these lords of
Tenuxtitlan, and the Indians under them, displayed in con-
structing the said bridge ; I can only say that it is the most
wonderful thing that ever was seen.

All the men and horses once out of the lagoon, we came
up, as it was feared, to a large morass, which lasted for three
arrow throws, the most frightful thing that man ever saw,
unsaddled horses sinking into it in such manner that at
times their ears only could be seen ; the more the poor
beasts tried to get out of it, the deeper they sank into the
mire, so that we soon lost all hope of saving any of them
or even passing ourselves ; yet by dint of perseverance and
work we contrived to put under them certain bundles of
grass, and light branches of trees, whereupon they might
support themselves so as not to sink altogether, by which
operation they were somewhat relieved. We were thus engaged going backwards and forwards to the assistance of our
horses, when fortunately for us a narrow channel of water
and mud was discovered, in which the beasts began at
once to move and swim a little, so that with the help of God
they all came out safe, though so fatigued from the constant
exertion that they could hardly stand on their feet. We all
offered many thanks to our Supreme Lord for the immense
favour received at his hands, for it is certain that without
his merciful assistance we should all have perished on the
spot, men and horses.

We had scarcely crossed the morass when we were met
by the Spaniards whom I had sent forward to Aculan,
bringing with them about eighty Indians, natives of that province, laden with provisions of every kind, maize, fowls, and
so forth. God only knows the joy we felt at sight of these
good things, especially at hearing that the Indians of Aculan
were peaceably inclined, and had shown no inclination to
desert their villages. With those Indians came two men of

some authority among them, who professed to have been
sent by a chief named Apaspolon,[1] with a message to me,
purporting how pleased he was with my intended visit to
his dominions ; that he already knew who I was, through
merchants of Tabasco and Xiculango travelling in those
parts, and that he would be delighted to make my acquaint-
ance ; finally, that he sent me some gold,.which his people
produced.

I received the gold, and told them to thank their chief
in my name for his goodwill towards me, as well as for the
readiness he showed for your Majesty's service. I bestowed
on them a few trifles, and dismissed them, in company with
the very Spaniards whom they had guided to the spot, all
seeming very happy and pleased. They however showed
their admiration of the bridge, and highly praised its
structure, which circumstance contributed in no small
degree to the confidence we afterwards placed in them ; for
their country lying among lakes and morasses, they might
easily, if they chose, hide themselves or escape through
them ; but when they saw the wonderful structure of that
bridge, they calculated that there was nothing we could not
achieve.

About this time an Indian messenger arrived from the
town of St. Esteban del Puerto, on the river of Panuco,
bringing me letters from the governors and alcaldes of those
parts. He was accompanied by four or five other Indians,
who also brought letters from this city of Tenuxtitlan, and
from Medellin, and from the town of Espiritu Santo. This
gave me much satisfaction, seeing by the contents of the
letters that they were all doing well, though I had no news
either of the factor Gonzalo de Salazar, or of the veedor
Peralmindez, whom, as I said before, I had despatched from
the town of Espiritu Santo, to settle the differences between
the treasurer and accounting-master, and if possible make

----
[1] The Vienna copy calls him Cupaspolon.

them friends ; for not having reached this city at the time the letters were written, these naturally said nothing about their doings.

The day after the Indians and Spaniards sent to Aculan had taken their departure, I with the rest of my people began to march in that direction. I passed the night on the mountain, and on the following day, about the hour of noon, came to the nearest plantations and farms in the province of Aculan. We were, however, still separated from them by a large morass, the crossing of which gave us some trouble, though we succeeded at last by making a detour of nearly one league, and leading our horses by the bridle. About the hour of vespers we arrived at the first village, called Tiçatepelt,[1] the inhabitants of which we found very comfortably established in their houses, without showing the least sign of fear. They had plenty of food for men as well as horses, so that we were completely refreshed, and soon forgot all past troubles.

I stayed six days at that village of Tiçatepelt, and was visited by a young Indian of prepossessing appearance, with a good train of followers, who said he was the son of the lord of that country, and presented me with some gold and birds, offering besides to place his person and estate at your Majesty's command. This youth further told me that his father had lately died, and I accordingly showed him sympathy for his loss, though I was persuaded he was telling me an untruth. I then gave him a necklace of Flanders beads which I was wearing at the time and he very much prized, after which I dismissed him, and he went away after remaining two whole days by me of his own free will.

One of the natives of Tiçatepelt, who professed to be the chief of the place, having told me that there was in the neighbourhood another village, also belonging to him, whereat I could find better lodgings and more abundant

[1] Tizatepel in the Vienna MS.

food—the village itself being larger and more populous—
and hinting besides that if I went thither I should be
more at ease, I at once accepted his proposal, and ordered
him to have the road cleared by his men, and lodgings prepared against our arrival. Everything was done as I
wished, and we reached without difficulty that second
village, which was distant about five leagues from the first.
We also found the people there in a state of great tranquillity, and a portion of the place already destined for our
lodging.

This village is very pretty, and is called Teutiercar[1] by
the natives. There are in it very handsome mosques or
idol-houses, where we took up our abode, casting out their
gods, at which the natives showed no great discontent,
owing no doubt to my having formerly spoken to them, and
given them to understand the error in which they lived,
telling them how there is one only God, creator of all
things. I again had an opportunity of speaking on this
subject to the principal chief, and to all of his people
assembled, and he told me that one of those two mosques
or idol-houses where we were lodging, and which was the
largest, was dedicated to a goddess, in whom they placed all
their faith and hopes, and that whenever they sacrificed to
her they chose very beautiful virgins, because if they were
not such she became very angry with them. That for this
reason they always took special care to procure such
as the goddess might accept and be pleased with them;
and that whenever a female child was found possessing
beauty of form and a pretty face, she was immediately taken
away from her parents, and brought up for that express
purpose.

On the subject of this nefarious practice and horrible
cruelty, in which the devil with his usual perversity and
art kept them entangled as in a thick net, I failed not to

[1] Elsewhere Teutiercas or Teutacras.

tell them what I considered necessary for their salvation.
They listened to me attentively, and seemed somewhat convinced by what they heard from my lips.

The chief of the village treated me with great friendliness,
and had long conversations with me, giving me a long and
detailed account of the Spaniards in whose quest I travelled, and of the road I was to take to find them. He declared to me in a mysterious manner that Apospolon, the
supreme lord of all that province, was still alive, though he
had ordered his own people to say that he was dead. He
begged and entreated me not to mention him as having been
my informant, because. he said he might suffer from it. The
young man who came to see me at Tiçatepelt was, in fact,
the son of Apospolon, but his father had given him instructions to endeavour to put me and my people out of
the direct way in order that we might not see the country
and villages under his rule. He gave me this information
out of friendship, and because, he was grateful for the favours
received at my hands ; but he again entreated me not to
reveal the matter to anyone, because, were Apospolon to know
that he was my informant, he would immediately put him
to death and set fire to his village.

I thanked the chief for his information, gave him a few
trifles, and promised to keep his secret, as he wished me to
do, and to reward in future the service he had rendered to
your Majesty. I then sent for the son of the lord, and told
him how much I wondered at his father having refused to
come and see me, knowing my good intentions towards them
all, and my wish to do them honour, and give them of what
I had by me in payment of their good reception, and of the
favours they had dispensed on me. I added that I knew
for certain that his father was alive, and that it was by his
express orders that he had reported him as dead, and therefore begged him to go and bring him back to me, for certainly he would be much benefited by so doing. The youth

acknowledged that his father was alive, and that if he had
given him out as dead, it was at his own express desire. He
would go to him forthwith, and do all he could to bring him
back : being confident of success, because his father had
already heard a great deal about me, and knew that I had
not come thither to do him harm, but on the contrary, to
give him and his people of such trifles as I carried with me.
He would have come already, only that, as he had given
himself out as dead, he felt somewhat ashamed of appearing
in my presence.

I again begged the youth to go and try what he could do.
He went, and returned the day after accompanied by his
father, who made me his excuses, saying that, not knowing
what my object was in coming to his estates, he had thought
it prudent to deny himself; but now that he was acquainted
with my motives for visiting his country, he was very glad
to see me. He had, it is true, through fear of me, instructed
his son to guide me by another route, away from his villages ;
but now he begged that I would go to the capital of his
states, where he resided, and where he could find greater
facilities to provide me and my people with anything we
might require.

Having made this offer, which I accepted, he gave orders
that a wide road should be opened, whilst he remained in my
company. We started the day after, and I gave him one of
my horses to ride by my side, and he went on very happy
and contented till we came to a village called Içancanac,[1]
which is very large and full of mosques.[2] It stands on a
large gulf or lagoon, which traverses the country as far as
the ports of Terminos, Xiculango, and Tabasco. Some of its
inhabitants had fled ; others were in their houses. We found
there plenty of provision, and Apospolon stayed with me in the
very rooms prepared for my lodging, though he had close by

---

[1] Another copy Cancanas.
[2] See above, p. 25, and note.

a house of his own, well provided with everything, and inhabited. As long as I remained at Içancanac he was particularly useful to me, giving me information about the
Spaniards in search of whom I came, and pointing out to me
on a piece of cloth the road that I was to follow. He moreover gave me some gold and women, without my asking for
them; I declare that on no occasion whatever have I asked
the lords and chiefs of these parts to give me anything,
unless they of their own aeccord and free will offered it.

To prosecute my journey it was necessary to cross the
above-mentioned lagoon, and before coming to it a morass.
Apospolon caused a bridge to be thrown over this, and provided me also with canoes for the crossing of the former. He
gave me besides guides for the road, and another set of
them in a canoe to conduct the Spaniard who had brought
me the letters and message from St. Esteban del Puerto,
as well as several canoes for the Indians who were returning
to Mexico, and to the provinces of Tabasco and Xiculango.
I gave that Spaniard letters for the authorities of the different towns, and for the lieutenants whom 1 had left in this
city of Tenuxtitlan, to govern in my absence, and for the
masters of the ships that were at Tabasco, and for the
Spaniards who were to come with the provisions, giving instructions to all and every one of them as to what they were
to do.

This being done, I gave Apospolon some few trifles which
he seemed to fancy, and leaving him contented, and all his
country peaceably settled and secure, I started from that
province of Aculan on the first Sunday of Lent of the year
1525. That day we did nothing but cross the lagoon, which
was no small matter. I ought to say that, at his own request I gave Apospolon a letter, in order that if any
Spaniards were to come that way they might know that
I had passed through his estates, and considered him as my
friend.

In the said province of Aculan an event occurred of which it is well that your Majesty should be informed. A good citizen of Tenuxtitlan, whose name was Mexicalçingo, but who received on his baptism that of Christoval, came to me one night in great secrecy, bringing with him certain drawings on a sheet of the paper used in that country. Having proceeded to explain to me the meaning of the figures on that paper, he said to me that Guatemucin,[1] formerly lord of Tenuxtitlan, and whom ever since the taking of this city I have kept a prisoner in my hands, on account of his rebellious nature and restless disposition—taking him with me wherever I went, as well as all the other chiefs and lords whom I thought cause of insecurity and revolt in this country—was endeavouring to form a conspiracy against me. The said Christoval explained how Guatemucin, and Guanacaxin,[2] the lord of Tescuco, and Tetepangueçal, the lord of Tacuba, and a certain Tacatelz,[3] who was at that time residing in this city of Mexico, in the territory of Tatelulco,[4] had often told him, Mexicalçingo or Christoval, how sad it was to be deprived of their personal estates, and of their power, by the Spaniards, and that they ought to find means of recovering their former possessions. That having consulted together many a time during the march, as to the best way of gaining their object, they had come to the conclusion that the best thing to do was to assassinate me and all the Spaniards who accompanied me, after which they might easily induce the natives of those provinces to rise, and marching against Christoval de Olid and his men, slay them all. This being accomplished, they would despatch their messengers to this city of Tenuxtitlan, inciting the people to rise and kill all

---

[1] Otherwise called Guatemozin, and Guateumezin. One of the copies has Guatamuzax.

[2] Guanacincen, *señor de Tasaico*, in other copies.

[3] Perhaps Tacatelt, which seems a more Mexican termination. I find his name written also Tacatele and Tacitecle.

[4] Tlatelulco.

the Spaniards, a thing which they flattered themselves might
be easily achieved, owing to their being for the most part
newly arrived and untrained to war. After this they would
raise the country, and order a general slaughter of the
Spaniards throughout the villages and towns, so that none
might escape; and they would moreover place strong garrisons
at all the seaports, so that no vessel coming from Castile could
return thither and carry back the news. In this manner
they flattered themselves they would again become lords and
masters of the country, as they were before our arrival; and
they felt so sure of their affair that they had already divided
between them the various provinces of the empire, allotting
one of them to the said Mexicalçingo (Christoval), my in-
former, as his share.

When I heard of this horrible plot framed against my
life and that of my Spaniards, I thanked God for having
thus revealed it to me through that worthy Indian. Early
in the morning of the next day I ordered all those Mexican
lords who had come in my suit to be arrested, and had them
placed each in one room, away from one another, so that
they might not communicate. I then went to see them
one by one, and interrogated them about the plot, pretending
that I had been informed by one of the conspirators; and as
they were kept in separate rooms, and could not speak to
each other, I managed to get out of them the real truth.
They owned that the principal authors of the conspiracy
were Guatemucin and Tetepanguecal, and that the others
knew also of the plot, but had refused to enter into it.

Having thus ascertained that the two above-mentioned
lords were the most guilty in this affair, I sentenced them
to be hung, and they were immediately executed. The
others I set at liberty, considering that their only crime consisted in having listened to their proposals, although this
circumstance alone was in my opinion sufficient for them to
deserve death. Their case, however, remains open, in order

that if ever they relapse they may be punished accordingly ;
although it is not likely they will, because so frightened
were they at the summary manner in which I treated the
whole affair, and so puzzled to know how I came to discover
the plot—they having never to this day guessed who was
my informant—that they firmly believe me in possession of
some wonderful art, by means of which I obtain the knowledge of hidden things.   Having observed that in order to
find out my way in these untrodden regions I from time to
time refer to a sea map and needle, as was the case at Çago-
tespan, they imagined that by help of that map and needle
I came to discover their secret.   So convinced are they of
this, that whenever they wished to testify their good will
they came to me begging I would consult the mirror and the
needle, in order to see whether their intentions were as good
as they professed, sure as they all were that through that
instrument I acquired the knowledge of the most hidden
and secret things.   This conviction of theirs I found so
useful for the future, that I never tried to disabuse them,
but on the contrary, strengthened their belief that the sea-
needle and map were the means I had of finding out all
things.

This province of Aculan is very large and thickly populated.   It has many villages, some of which were visited by
my Spaniards.   It abounds in honey and food of various
kinds.   There are in it many merchants, who trade in different
parts, and are rich in slaves and other articles of commerce.   Aculan is entirely surrounded by lagoons, every
one of which communicates with the bay and port called
Los Terminos, through which they carry on by water
a considerable trade with Xiculango[1] and Tabasco.   It is
through those lagoons that they are supposed to reach that
other sea, the country called Yucatan being thus made a

---

[1] Some of the copies have Cicalcingo, which seems to me an erroneous
reading.

complete island. But this is only a report; I will endeavour
to ascertain the truth of it, so as to inform your Majesty
at full length.

As far as I could learn, there is no other lord in the
whole province of Aculan but this Apospolon, of whom I
have already told your Majesty. He is the richest of the
traders of this country, and has more ships at sea. He
carries on his commerce far off, and at Nito, a town of
which I will say more hereafter, and where I met some of
the Spaniards belonging to Gil Gonzales de Avila's suit,
there is a whole suburb filled with his agents, and among
them one of his own brothers, who manages the whole concern. The chief articles of trade in those provinces consist
of cacao, cotton-cloth, colours for dyeing, and a species of
tint, with which they besmear their bodies all over to guard
against heat and cold; candlewood, to light themselves;
aromatic resin, extracted from the pine tree, for the incen-
sing of their idols; slaves; and lastly, certain red beads,
which differ from coral, and are held in great estimation
by the natives, who ornament their persons with them
in their festivals and carousals. They also deal in gold,
though in small quantities, and mixed either with copper or
with other metals.

To this Apospolon, as well as to other worthy natives of
this province, who came to visit me, I failed not to open my
mind about their idols, informing them as I had done before
with others, of what they were to believe in order to ensure
the future salvation of their souls, and how they were to
conduct themselves in the service of your Majesty. They
listened to me with attention, seemed gratified at what I
told them, and burned many of their idols in my very
presence, declaring that they would no longer worship
them, but would obey any commands I might be pleased to
give them in your Majesty's name. Upon which I took leave
of them, and continued my journey, as aforesaid.

Three days before my departure from the province of Aculan, I sent forward four Spaniards, with two guides that Apospolon procured me, that they might look out for a road to the neighbouring province of Maçatlan—which in the language of the natives is called Quiniacho.[1] I had been told by the said Apospolon that on my way thither I should have to cross a great desert, and pass four nights in the midst of forests, and therefore I gave the men instructions, and told them to inspect the ground well, and report to me whether there would be any morasses or rivers to pass. From fear, however, of such hardships and hunger as we had to go through at Çagoatespan, I gave orders that all my people should take food for six days. This being done, and my people amply supplied with the necessaries of life—for they had in that place abundance of every thing—I started on my journey. Five leagues beyond a certain lagoon, which we crossed, I met the four Spaniards, who, guided by the two natives, had gone in search of a road. They told me there was a very good one, although completely girded by forests; that it was level, and without any rivers or morasses to cross. They further added that they had come up to a certain spot in the said province of Maçatlan, whence they had seen plantations and even some of the natives, and they came back unnoticed by them.

I was delighted to hear this news, and ordered six of my men on foot to go forwards with some of our Indian friends, and keep always one league in advance of those who were opening the road, in order that if they came upon any travellers or stray Indians they might seize and stop them, enter the province without being observed, and thus prevent the inhabitants from deserting their dwellings and setting fire to their villages, as others before them had done. That very day, close to a water lake, my people seized two Indians, who professed to be natives of the province of Aculan, and

[1] Elsewhere Quiacho and even Quiatlco.

said they were coming from that of Maçatlan, where they had lately been bartering salt for cotton clothing. This account of their persons seemed probable enough, for they were laden with that article. Being brought to my presence, and asked whether in the province whence they came there was any rumour about us, they answered there was not, and that the inhabitants were in a perfect state of tranquillity. I then told them that they must needs return thither with me, but not to be frightened at it, for they would not lose any thing of what they carried, but on the contrary, I would give them of what I had with me ; and, moreover, upon our arrival at the province of Maçatlan they would be allowed to go away ; that I was a great friend of all the natives of Aculan, because they and their lord had been very kind to me. The men did with perfect goodwill what I asked from them, and guided us by another road, that taken by my Spaniards leading only to certain farms or plantations, whereas theirs brought us to the very centre of their villages.

The night of that day was passed in the forest. The day after the Spaniards, who went forwards as pioneers, met four Indians, natives of Maçatlan, with their bows and arrows, who were upon the road as sentries or scouts. On the approach of our people, the Indians shot their arrows, and wounded one of our men ; but they fled and were hotly pursued. Owing, however, to the thickness of the forest, our people could only secure one of the fugitives, whom they placed in the hands of three of our Indians, whilst the Spaniards followed the pursuit, thinking there were more enemies in the wood. But no sooner were the Spaniards out of sight, than some of the fugitives, who, as it afterwards appeared, lay hidden in the bushes, came back to the spot, and, falling upon our three Indian friends, fought with them and released the prisoner. Ashamed at their defeat, the Indians followed their enemies across the forest, and having overtaken them, fought with them, and wounded one in the arm by a great sword-cut, taking him prisoner; the others took to flight, especially as they heard some of our people approach.

I asked that prisoner whether his countrymen knew of my coming, and he answered they did not; I then inquired for what purpose he and his companions had been watching. His answer was that such was their habit, being then at war with some of their neighbours, and that the lord of the land, providing for the security of his people, who were then occupied in their field labours, had watch-guards stationed on the different roads to prevent any surprise. Having then ascertained from him that the first village of that province was close by, I made all possible haste in order to arrive there before any of his companions, the fugitive Indians, should give the alarm; and I ordered those of my people who went in front to halt as soon as they came in sight of the plantations, to hide themselves in the forest, and wait until my arrival. When I came to the appointed place it was already late in the day. I hastened on my march, thinking we might reach the village that very night; but perceiving that the Indians who carried our luggage and provisions were somewhat spread and scattered, I ordered a captain with twenty horsemen to remain at the plantations, collect the carriers as they came on, and pass the night there, after which all together were to follow me. For my own part, I took a narrow path through the forest: it was level and straight enough, though so shut up by trees on either side that I could hardly cut my way through it. I walked on foot and led my horse, all my people behind me doing the same. In this manner we marched until night came on, when we were stopped by a morass, which could not be traversed without being previously fitted for the passage of the men. Seeing this, I gave orders, which were quickly transmitted from one man to another, to return to a small hut which we had passed in the evening, and there we spent the night, although without water for ourselves or our horses.

In the morning of the next day, having had the morass strewed with branches of trees and made fit for our passage, we cleared it, though with some difficulty, leading our horses by the hand. Three leagues beyond the spot where we had passed the night we perceived a village perched on a rock. Thinking that we had not been noticed, I approached it with great precaution, and found it so completely surrounded [by palisades] that we could not for a time find an entrance to it. At last we discovered one, and went in; but found the village deserted, though full of provisions of every sort, such as maize, fowls, honey, beans, and other produce of the land; for as the inhabitants of the place were taken by surprise, they had no time to remove any of their stores, which were abundant, owing to their village being a frontier one.

The village is situated, as I said before, upon a high rock; it has a great lake on one side, and on the other a deep stream that throws itself into the lake. It has but one accessible entrance, and is surrounded by a deep moat, behind which is a wooden palisade reaching as high as a man's breast, and behind this palisade a kind of breast-work made of thick boards, ten feet[1] high, with its embrasures all along to shoot out arrows, and watchtowers rising seven or eight feet more above the said wall, which was also flanked by round towers having large stones on the top to throw on the assailants. All the houses in the village were strengthened in a like manner and loopholed, and the streets barricaded in the most scientific and effective manner possible considering their mode of warfare and the weapons they use.

From this place I dispatched some of my people in various

---

[1] The original here has *de hasta dos estados de altura. Estado* being sometimes used in old Spanish to designate a man's height, I have calculated it at five feet.

directions in search of natives whom I might interrogate.
They succeeded in bringing me two or three, whom I sent,
accompanied by one of those Indian pedlars from Aculan, in
search of the lord of the place. They were to tell him, in
my name, not to be frightened at my coming, but to return
to his village, for I did not come to do him or his people
any harm, but on the contrary to help him, if necessary, in
his wars against his neighbours, so as to leave his country
in a state of perfect security.

Two days after this the messengers came back, bringing
with them an uncle of the lord of the land, who was then
governing in his nephew's name, he being too young for the
task. Fear, it was alleged, had prevented his coming. I spoke
to the uncle, and restored his confidence, upon which he
conducted me to another village of the same province, called
Tiax,[1] about seven leagues further on. This was much
larger than the former, and equally well fortified, though
not so strong, being situated on a plain. It had, like the
other village, strong pallisades, a deep moat, and watch towers.
Each of the three suburbs or quarters into which it was
divided had a strong wall, and the whole was encircled by
an outer one, stronger than the rest.

I had sent on to this village two companies of horse
and another one of foot, each under a captain; but upon
arrival they found the place entirely deserted, though full
of provisions. My men, however, contrived to secure
close by seven or eight of the natives, some of whom they
afterwards set at liberty, that they might go and speak to
their chief, and quiet the people. In this they succeeded so
well, that before my arrival at the place its chief had
already sent his messengers with some provision and cotton
clothing as a present. During our stay in that town the
natives again returned, bringing food and peaceably conversing with us; but this time they were not sent only by

_____
[1] Also written at times Tiar, Tiacle, and even Tiac.

that chief, but by five or six more in the immediate neighbourhood, who were all independent of each other. Every
one of these chiefs offered himself as the vassal of your
Majesty, and promised to be our friend, though I never could
persuade them to come and see me. As I had not much
time to spare, I sent each of them a verbal message, purporting that I accepted their vassalage in your Majesty's name,
and begging them to procure me guides to prosecute my
journey, which they did of very good will, giving me one
who not only was well acquainted with the countries I had
to traverse, but had even visited them, and seen the very
Spaniards in search of whom I came. I therefore, took my
departure from Tiac, and passed the night at another village,
called Yasuncabil,[1] which is the last of that province. I
found it deserted, and surrounded by pallisades, as were the
other two. Its chief had a most beautiful residence,
though it was built entirely of straw. We there provided
ourselves with every thing necessary for our journey, our
guide having told us that we should find a desert of five
leagues before we reached the province of Taiza,[2] which we
had to traverse; and so it proved to be in reality.

Here, in the province of Maçatlan, or Quiniacho, as it is
otherwise called, I dismissed the two pedlars I had stopped
on the road, as well as the guides from Aculan, giving to
each of them some small trifles, besides other things which
they were to present in my name to their respective lords,
upon which they all went away very happy and contented.
The chief of the first village in this province, who had
accompanied me, I also dismissed at this spot, allowing him
to take away with him some of his women who had been

[1] The Vienna copy Iiasmicabil, and even Tiasmicabil. Tiac is again
written here Tiacle.
[2] Elsewhere Taiça, Tahiça, and even Yaiza; but perhaps Itza is
meant, which really was the name of that province.

captured by my men in the forest. I also gave him a small present, at which he seemed very much pleased.

Once out of the province of Maçatlan, I directed my steps towards that of Taiza. I slept four nights on the road, all that country being inhabited. My way was over rocky mountains of considerable height ; and I had to traverse a very dangerous pass, which being formed of very fine alabaster, I named *Puerto del Alabastro.*

On the fifth day of our march, the pioneers, who went in front with the guide, came to a great lake, looking like an arm of the sea. So large and deep it is, that although its waters are sweet, I am of opinion that it really forms part of the ocean.[1] There was on it a small island, and in the island a village, which the guide said was the chief place in the province of Taiza, and that if we wished to go there, we could only do it in canoes. Hearing this, the Spaniards remained on the bank of the lake keeping watch, whilst one of them came back to me and reported ; upon which I ordered my men to halt, and went thither on foot that I might examine the lake and its situation. Upon my arrival on the spot, I found that my pioneers had succeeded in securing one Indian belonging to that village on the island, who had come on shore in a very small boat, for the purpose

---

[1] I need scarcely observe that Cortes was wrong in supposing that this lake communicated with the sea. It is, however, very large, the section of it where the town of Flores now stands measuring three leagues in length by one half in breadth, whereas the larger portion is twelve leagues long. It was called by the natives *Nohuken,* a word meaning great drinker, to express, no doubt, the great mass of water accumulated in its basin. Ancient Spanish chroniclers call it indifferently *laguna de Peten, de Lacandones,* or *de el Itza,* which last denomination seems the most acceptable, as conveying the notion of the primitive inhabitants. About the beginning of the fifteenth century the dynasty reigning over Yucatan was overthrown, its capital city, Mayapan, was destroyed, and the Itzaes coming from the south took possession of the territories adjoining the lake. See Cogolludo, *Historia de Chiapa, Yucatan, etc.*

of reconnoitring. He was armed, and though surprised
by my people, he would have escaped had not a dog of
ours overtaken and seized him before he threw himself
into the water.

From this Indian I learned that his countrymen knew
nothing about my arrival. I asked him whether there was
any means of reaching the village on the island, and he
answered there was none ; but that not far from the spot
there was a narrow arm of that lake, on the other side of
which we should find some plantations and houses, and that
if we managed to arrive there without being seen we were
sure to have canoes. Hearing this, I sent order to my people
to advance, and taking ten or twelve archers with me, I
followed on foot the road which that Indian had pointed out
to me. We had to cross a rather long morass, intersected by
pools, in which the water reached to our waists and sometimes higher up. In this manner we came to the plantations,
but as the road was bad, and we could not always conceal
our march, we were seen from a distance. On our arrival
the inhabitants of the place were taking hastily to their
canoes in order to escape by the lake. I marched on the
banks for about two-thirds of a league, across plantations
and by houses, but everywhere we had been perceived,
and the inhabitants were paddling off in their canoes.
As it was late in the day, and I considered it a useless
task to follow the fugitives, I ordered my people to halt
and encamp at those plantations, taking such military
precautions as were in my power ; having been told by the
guide from Maçatlan that the people about this lake were
the most numerous and warlike of all their neighbours,
and much dreaded in consequence. My guide then proposed to take that little canoe in which the Indian had
come, and make for the small island in the lake, which could
be seen at a distance of about two leagues. He was well

acquainted with the chief, whose name was Canec,[1] and he
would speak to him, and tell him what my intentions were,
and the object of my coming to his country, since he knew
them well, having accompanied me part of the way. He
had no doubt the chief would listen to his words and believe
in them, and allow his fears to be calmed, for he knew him
intimately, having several times visited the village on the
island, and stayed at his house.

This proposition of the guide seemed to me a very
excellent one. I accepted his offer, gave him the canoe and
the Indian who had come from the island, and told him
that if he succeeded in his undertaking I would reward
him to his heart's content. He went away, and about
midnight returned to me, bringing with him two worthy
citizens of that village, who came in the chief's name to
ascertain the truth of the guide's report, and inquire
what I wanted of him. I received them well, gave them
some of the trifles I had with me, and informed them that
my arrival in those regions was by your Majesty's express
commands, and for the mere purpose of gaining a knowledge
of the country and its inhabitants, and communicating with
the lords and chiefs of the land on matters touching the
royal service and their own welfare. They were to invite
the chief to come and see me without fear ; and if he hesi-
tated, to propose that one of my Spaniards should go and
remain on the island as an hostage all the time the chief
was with me. With this message they went back accompanied by the guide and by one of the Spaniards. The day
after the chief himself arrived, escorted by about thirty men
in five or six canoes, and bringing with him the Spaniard
I had given him as a hostage. He seemed much pleased

---

[1] The same individual called Kanec by Villagutierre and Cogolludo.
But Cortes here, as well as the two mentioned writers, mistook the title
of the chief for his name, *canec* in the dialect of the Itzaes meaning the
same thing as *cacique* among the Mexicans.

at seeing me, and I received him with a great show of affection.

It happened that when this chief and his people presented themselves in our camp it was the hour of mass. I ordered one to be chaunted with great solemnity, and with the usual accompaniment of clarions and sackbuts. He heard it with great composure, and watched attentively all the ceremonies of divine service. The mass over, the Franciscan friars I had with me came on, and one of them preached a sermon, which being translated by the interpreter, could very well be understood by the chief and his people, wherein he informed them of all things touching our faith, and gave them to understand, by a series of arguments, how there was but one only God, and how all those who followed their sect were sure to be damned. The chief shewed much satisfaction at what he heard, declaring that his wish was immediately to destroy all his idols, and to believe in that God of whom we had spoken to him ; but that he wanted to be told in what way he was to honour and worship him. That if I chose to accompany him to his village, I would soon have occasion to see how he ordered all the idols to be burnt in my presence ; and he moreover begged me to leave him one of those crosses, which I was in the habit of planting wherever I went.

The sermon and conference over, I again spoke to the chief, and told him about your Majesty's greatness, and how he and all living creatures were the natural subjects and vassals of your Imperial Highness, and bound to your service. That to those who did so, your Majesty granted all manner of favours, which I, in the royal name, had already dispensed, wherever I had been, to all those who had willingly offered to be the vassals of your Majesty, and placed themselves under your Imperial rule. The same, or greater, I promised to him if he followed their example.

His answer was that he never to that moment had

acknowledged a superior, nor had he been told that there was one to obey. True it was that about five or six years before some of the people of Tabasco, coming through his country, had informed him how a certain captain, followed by men of our nation, had come among them, and had vanquished them in three pitched battles. The same people had likewise told him that they were to become henceforwards the vassals of a great lord, and many other things similar to those which I was now telling him. He, therefore, wished to know whether the supreme lord to whom I was now referring was the same to whom the men of Tabasco had alluded.

I answered him that I was the captain who had passed through Tabasco, and that it was I who had fought with them. That if they wished to know whether I told them the truth or not, they had only to ask that interpreter who was then by my side, an Indian woman, native of that country, whose name, after christening, was Marina. She had been presented to me with twenty other girls by the people of Tabasco, and had accompanied me ever since. This woman, therefore, spoke to the chief, and told him it was perfectly true that I had conquered Mexico, and she enumerated one by one all the lands and provinces that are at present subjected and obedient to your Majesty's imperial rule.

This being heard by the chief, he shewed his contentment at it, and said he was ready to become at once the subject and vassal of your Majesty, and that he considered himself fortunate to obey so powerful a prince as I told him your Highness was. After this he sent for fowls and honey, and some gold, and certain beads made of red shells, which they very much prize, and made me a present of all that. I, in return, gave him of the things I carried with me, at which he shewed his contentment, and he afterwards dined with me, being very much pleased at the reception I gave him.

The dinner being over, I informed him how I was travel-

ling in search of certain Spaniards who were on the sea
coast, because they formed part of my army, and had been
sent by me to those distant parts; it was a very long time
since I had news of them, and for that reason I was going
in search of them, and therefore begged him to give me
such information as he might possess respecting them. The
chief said in answer that he knew a great deal about my
countrymen, because not far from the spot where they were
settled, he had certain vassals of his, who took care of a
plantation of chocolate trees, the country being very favourable to their growth. From these, as well as from numerous
traders, who frequently went to and fro, he continually received news of them; he would procure me guides who
knew the country well, and would conduct me and my men
to the very residence of the Spaniards. The road thither
however was a bad one, leading through a rough and
mountainous country, full of rocks and precipices, so that if
I could go by sea it would be much better for me. I told
him that, followed as I was by such numbers, and with so
many horses and such heavy luggage I could never find
canoes enough to go by water, and therefore was compelled,
as he saw, to travel by land. I asked him, however, to give
me the means of crossing that lake; upon which he said to
me that about three leagues from the spot where we then
were the water of the lake became suddenly very shallow,
and dried up, and that by coasting it I could return to the
road opposite his village; but he begged and hoped, that
since my people were going round the lake, I, at least,
should accompany him in his canoe and visit his village
and house, where I might witness the burning of the idols,
and order a cross to be made for him. To be agreeable to
that chief, though against the advice of my own people, I
accepted his offer, and having embarked with about twenty
of my suite—most of them archers—accompanied him to his

village,[1] where I spent the rest of that day in pleasure.
When night came on I took leave of the chief, and under the
guidance of a native he gave me, entered the canoes, and
landed at a spot on the shore where I found already most of
my people encamped, and where we passed the night.

At this village, or rather at the plantations that were close
to the lake, I was obliged to leave one of my horses, owing
to his having got a splinter in his foot. The chief promised
to take care of the animal and cure him, but I do not know
that he will succeed, or what he will do with him.[2]

On the following day, after collecting together the people,
I started, preceded by the guides, and about one half a
league's distance from the spot whereat we had encamped,
came up to a small plain and huts, and thence to a hill of

---

[1] This chief, or *canec*, inhabited an island called Tayasal. When, in
1697, the Spaniards under Don Martin de Ursua took definitive possession of that country—all previous attempts having failed—they changed
its name into *Nuestra Señora de los Remedios y San Pablo;* but this
singular denomination has since become obsolete, and it is now generally
called *Remedios-Peten.* This may perhaps be a proper place to observe
that the word *peten* means a lake, and the whole of that country was in
old times, and I believe is still now, known as *Peten-Itza.* The town,
where the chief himself resided, must have been very large, since it
contained twenty-one *adoratorios* or idol-houses. When the Spaniards
conquered the island, they found it so strewed with places of worship
and stone idols, that from seven in the morning to six in the evening
they were occupied, without taking any rest, in breaking and destroying
them.

[2] About this horse of Cortes a very curious anecdote is told by Villagutierre. He says that when the Franciscan friars who accompanied
Ursua's expedition in 1697 entered the island, and were looking for
a convenient spot to make of it a place of worship, they came upon
a large temple, and found inside the image of a horse tolerably well
executed in freestone. Having made inquiries about it, they were told
that the natives, out of compliment to Cortes, had raised the animal to
the rank of one of their gods, under the name of *Tziminchak*, after he
had died in consequence of the excessive care they took of him, and the
respect they had for Cortes; for it would appear that instead of giving
him proper forage, they had presented him with flowers and birds, which
of course the poor beast could not eat, and thereby was starved to death.

small elevation ; after which, at a distance of one league and
a half, we arrived again at some beautiful plains, covered
with grass, whence I sent forward some horse and foot, with
orders to stop and secure any natives they might find on
their way, our guides having told us that we should arrive
that very night at a village. Those plains we found to
abound in deer, and we hunted all that day on horseback,
and speared eighteen of them, though owing to the great
heat and to our horses being out of condition, our way having
hitherto been through mountainous or swampy districts, two
of them died from the exertion, and several more were in
great danger.

The hunting over, we proceeded on our road, and shortly
after, met some of our outrunners, who were waiting for us.
They had overcome and seized four Indian hunters, who had
just killed a lion and some iguanas—a species of large lizard
abounding in those islands. Having asked them whether at
their village they had any notion about me, they answered
they had not, and then pointed out to me the habitations or
farms whence they came, which were seen in the distance,
about one league and a half from the place where we then
stood. Thither I went in all haste, thinking I might arrive
without any difficulty, and before the inhabitants saw me ;
but when I thought I was about to enter the village, and
actually saw the people moving in it, we came upon a large
lagoon, which seemed to me too deep to be crossed, and I
therefore ordered my people to halt. As the village was not
far off, I began to make signs and call the inhabitants to me,
when two Indians in a canoe, with about one dozen fowls,
came very close to the place where I stood on horseback,
with the water to the girths ; but although I remained conversing with them a good while, and trying to persuade
them to approach the shore, they never would, through fear,
and began even to retreat towards their village. Seeing
which, one of the Spaniards who was on horseback by my

side spurred his steed through the waters, and swam after
them. The Indians were so frightened at the horse that they
jumped into the lagoon, and abandoned their canoe, upon
which some of my men, who were good swimmers, overtook
them, and brought them prisoners to the shore.

But whilst I was thus engaged the people had completely
deserted the village. I asked those Indians which way our
road was, and they pointed out to me a spot where by a cir-
cuitous march of about one league we should find convenient
passage, the lagoon being at that place almost dry. We followed their directions, and arrived the same night at the
village, and slept in it.

The name of this place is Checan;[1] it is eighteen leagues
distant from the spot whence we started, and is under a
chief named Amohan.[2] I stayed there four days, collecting
provisions for six more, having been told by the guides that
I should have to cross a desert of that length. I had
another reason for so long a delay. I wished to wait for
the chief of the village, for whom I had sent, he being absent
with the rest of the inhabitants when I entered the place.
But although I tried all means in my power to calm his fears,
and sent him several messages by those Indians I had taken,
neither he nor they ever came back.

Having, therefore, collected the most provision I could, I
started on my journey, and marched the first day through a
level and fine looking country, without wood, except now and
then a little, and at the end of six leagues we came to the foot of
a great mountain ridge, where, and close to a river, we found
a large house and two or three smaller ones, all surrounded
by maize plantations. The house, the guides told me, belonged to Amohan, the lord of Checan, who kept it as an inn

[1] Sometimes written Cheçan.

[2] The name of this chief is differently written in the various manu-
scripts, Almohan, Amochan, and Amohan, which last reading I have
adopted.

for the numerous traders passing that way. I stayed there one day besides that of my arrival, first because it happened to be a festival of the church, and secondly because I wished to give time to the pioneers, who went in front opening the road. In that river near Checan we had very excellent fishing, for we cut off and took a large quantity of shad, not one of those that entered the sluice having escaped.

The day after this, we marched seven leagues, through a rough and mountainous country, and passed the night on the banks of a large river. On the next, after about three leagues of very bad road, we came to a beautiful plain, without wood, except a few pine trees. In these plains, which extended for two leagues, we killed seven deer, and we dined on the banks of a very fresh stream that traverses them. After dinner we began to ascend a mountain pass, which though of no great elevation, was exceedingly steep and rough ; so much so, that although we led our horses by the hand, we had still considerable difficulty in the ascent. In coming down we found about half a league of level country, after which there was another mountain pass, which took us fully two hours and a half to go up and down. So bad and rough it was, that all the horses lost their shoes in it.

We passed that night at the bottom of the pass on the other side of the mountain, close to a small stream, where we remained all next day, nearly till the hour of vespers, attending to the shoeing of our horses ; for although there were in my small army two farriers, and about ten more men who helped in nail rivetting, the operation could not be finished in one day. I went on to sleep three leagues further, and left many of my men behind to attend to the horses and wait for the Indian carriers, who, owing to the bad roads, and to the heavy rains that fell, had necessarily remained behind.

The day after, having heard from the guides that close

upon my path there was a farm called Asuncapin[1] belonging
to the lord of Taiza, and that I could very well arrive early
in the evening, and pass the night there, I again took to
the road, and after marching four or five leagues more,
came to the said farm, which we found deserted. At this
place I stayed two days, for the purpose of collecting together the luggage carriers, and making provision ; which
being done, I set on, and went to sleep at another farm-
house, called Taxuitel,[2] distant about five leagues from the
former, and belonging also to Amohan, the lord of Checan.
It was well-planted with chocolate trees and maize, though
the latter fruit was but in small quantity, and too green to
be reaped.

I was here informed by the guides and by the manager of
the farm, whom we succeeded in taking prisoner, as well as
his wife and a son of his, that we should soon have to cross
a chain of high and rocky mountains, where there was
no habitation of any kind ; and that after this we should
arrive at other farms, belonging to Canec,[3] the lord of Taiza,
and bearing the name of Tenciz. We did not stay long at this
place, starting the day after our arrival. After traversing six[4]
leagues of level country we began to ascend the mountain
pass, which is one of the most wonderful things in the world
to behold ; for were I to attempt its description, and picture
to your Majesty its roughness, as well as the difficulties of
every kind we had to surmount, I should utterly fail in the
undertaking. I can, however, assure your Majesty that
neither I nor those who are more eloquent could find words
to give a proper idea of it ; even if we did, we could never

[1] Elsewhere Auecapin and Suncapin. One of the copies reads Hesu-
capin.

[2] Also written Taxuytel, Japuitel and Japitel, these latter readings
being occasioned by the similarity of the letters T and J as they were
written at the time.

[3] See above, p. 52.

[4] In another copy " two."

be understood except by those who saw it with their own
eyes, and experienced the fatigues and perils of the ascent.
It will be sufficient to inform your Majesty that we were
twelve days in making the eight leagues across the pass,
and that we lost on this occasion no less than sixty-eight of
our horses, that either fell down precipices or were ham-
strung and disabled by their fall. The rest arrived so fatigued
and hurt that scarcely one was of service to us, and three
months passed before any of them were fit for riding.[1] All
the time we were ascending this awful pass it never ceased
raining day and night, and yet the mountains we had to cross
were so shaped, having no crevices wherein the rain might
stop, that we had no water to drink, and were greatly tormented by thirst, most of our horses perishing through it.
Indeed, had it not been for some which we were able to
collect in copper kettles and other vessels, whilst encamping
at night in huts made for that purpose, no man or horse
could have escaped alive.

Whilst crossing this mountain pass, a nephew of mine fell
down and broke his leg in two or three places ; and after this
misfortune—which all of us deplored—we had the greatest
difficulty to carry him over to the other side in the state in
which he was.

But our dangers were not yet over. About one league
before we came to the farms of Tenciz,[2] which, as I said before, are on the other side of these mountains, we were
stopped by a large river, the waters of which were increased
and swollen beyond measure by the late rains, so that it
was impossible for us to cross it. The Spaniards sent in
advance to explore, finding no passage, had gone up the

[1] Bernal Diaz, who accompanied Cortes in this expedition, confirms
the statement, and gives a graphic account of the dangers attending the
ascent.

[2] The same place mentioned at p. 60, though here it is written Teneis,
and elsewhere Teucas.

stream and discovered the most wonderful ford that ever
had been seen or heard of; for the river at that particular
spot spreads for upwards of two-thirds of a league, owing
to certain large rocks which impede its course. Between
these rocks natural channels are formed, through which the
water runs with great rapidity and force, there being no
other possible outlet for the stream. By means of these
rocks, which fortunately lay close enough to each other, we
managed to pass that dangerous river, cutting down large
trees, which we laid across, and holding fast by *bejucos* or
pliable reeds thrown from one rock to another. Yet this
mode of crossing was so dangerous that had one of us become giddy or lost his foot he must inevitably have perished.
There were in the river more than twenty of these narrow
channels, so that it took us two whole days to cross it. The
horses swam across at a place lower down the river, where
the current was not so strong; but although the distance to
Tenciz was only one league, as I said before, they were
nearly three days in doing it; indeed, most of them were so
fatigued and broken down by their last march across the
mountains, that my men were almost obliged to carry them
on their shoulders, and even then they could not help themselves.

I arrived at Tenciz on the 15th day of May[1] of 1525, the
evening before Easter (Pascua de Resureccion), although
most of my men—especially those who had horses to attend
to—did not join me until three days after. I found on my
arrival that the Spaniards whom I had sent forward had preceded me by two days, and taken possession of two or three
of the above mentioned habitations or farms, securing about
twenty and odd Indians, who, unconscious of my presence
in those parts, had been taken unawares. Having asked

[1] The month is omitted, *a quince dias del año*, etc.; but Easter
having fallen for that year on the 16th of April, I have filled up the
blank accordingly.

them whether they had any provisions, they answered me that they had none, nor could they be procured for several leagues round, which news put us in the greatest possible consternation, and increased our wants beyond measure, since for the last ten days we had fed exclusively on cores of palm trees and palmettos, and these in small numbers, for we were so weak that we had scarcely strength enough to cut them down. I was, however, informed by one of their chiefs that about one day's march up the river, which had again to be crossed at the same dangerous spot, there was a well populated district, called Tahuytal[1] where I would find abundance of maize, cacao and fowls, and that he was ready to furnish me with a guide. I immediately sent one of my captains in that direction, with thirty Spaniards dismounted, and upwards of one thousand Indians of those who composed my train, when the Almighty permitted that they should find the country full of people, and great quantities of maize, with which we were not a little restored; although, the distance being great and the road very bad, the provisioning was not so regular as I might have wished.

From these plantations I sent forward some of my crossbowmen, accompanied by a guide of the country, with orders to explore the roads in the direction of a province called Acuculin, until they should come to a village which, according to my information, was ten leagues beyond the place where I was then encamped. The village was at a distance of six leagues from Acuculin, the chief town of the province of that name, and the lord of all that territory was Acahuilguin. My Spaniards arrived there unnoticed, and having entered by surprise one of the habitations, found seven men and one woman, with whom they returned to me, saying that, although the road they had taken was bad

[1] All copies agree in writing the name of this place Tahuytal, but it should be observed that at p. 60 a village called Tatahuytel is also mentioned.

and rough, it had appeared to them easy and good in comparison with those we had walked hitherto. From these Indian prisoners, whom I interrogated several times, I was able to collect information respecting the Spaniards in search of whom I was going. There was among them a native of the province of Aculan, who said he was a merchant, having his residence and carrying on his trade in the very town where my countrymen had established themselves; that the name of that town was Nito, and that considerable trade was carried on in it by merchants of all parts of the country; that the people of Aculan, to whom he himself belonged, inhabited a suburb of their own, and had as their chief a brother of Apospolon, the lord of Aculan; that the Christians had come there one night and taken possession of the town, and robbed the inhabitants of every thing they possessed, besides a good deal of valuable merchandise, for there were in the town traders from all parts. That in consequence of this inroad made by the Spaniards, which had occurred about a year before, the inhabitants had fled to other countries; and that he and certain brother merchants from Aculan had applied to, and obtained from, Acahuilguin, the lord of Acuculin, permission to establish themselves on his domain, and he had given them a spot of land where they had settled, building that small village, whence they carried on their traffic, though owing to the inroad of the Spaniards, and to their having taken possession of their town, trade was then very slack, as there was no other channel for it but that one, and merchants did not venture through it from fear of the strangers. That before reaching the spot where the said Spaniards were settled, I would have to cross over an extensive gulf or arm of the sea, and many a mountain of the worst kind, during ten days' march, but that if it was my pleasure, he would be my guide, as he knew the road well, and had visited the place many a time.

Delighted to have such a guide, I accepted his services, and treated him well, causing the guides I had brought from Maçatlan and Taiça to speak to him, and tell him how well I had behaved towards them, and how I was the great friend of their common lord, Apospolon. This had the effect of increasing the merchant's confidence to such a degree that I determined to release him and his companions, and trust entirely to them, dismissing at the same time the guides I had with me, after having presented them with a few trifles for themselves and their chiefs, and thanked them for their good services.

This being done, and the guides from Maçatlan and Taiça having departed, very much satisfied at the manner in which they had been treated, I ordered that four men from Acuculin, and two men chosen from among the inhabitants of Tenciz, should go forward with a message of mine to the lord of Acuculin, and persuade him to wait for my arrival. They were followed by other Indians, who made the road practicable for me and my small army, and I myself followed in the rear with the remainder of the force, though the difficulty of getting provisions, and the want of rest, both for man and beast, made me tarry at the place two days longer. We began our march at last, leading most of our horses, until we came to a place where we passed the night; but what was our astonishment to find, at break of the following day, that the man who was to act as my guide and those who remained with him had disappeared during the night! God only knows how affected I was by the mishap, finding myself without guides after having dismissed those I had brought from Maçatlan. I went on, however, and spent the night on a mountain, five leagues distant from that spot, where, owing to the roughness of the paths, another of my horses—the only one that still remained uninjured—was disabled by a fall, and at the moment I write has not yet entirely recovered. The next

day I marched six leagues, and crossed two rivers, one of them
by aid of a tree, which had accidentally fallen across the
stream, and was soon converted into a sort of bridge for our
passage, the horses being made to swim across, though two
mares were drowned in the attempt. The other river was
crossed in canoes, the horses swimming.

After this we arrived at a small village of about fifteen
newly-built houses, where we passed the night. I there
learned that the houses belonged to merchants of Aculan,
originally from the town where the Christians had settled. At
this village I stayed two days, in order to collect the men and
luggage that remained behind ; and this being accomplished,
I sent forward two troops of horse and a company of infantry
in the direction of Acuculin, which they reached without
accident. I soon received from them a written message,
stating that they had found the place completely deserted,
but that in a large house belonging to the lord of the land
they had taken two men, who were waiting there by the
command of their chief, to let him know of my arrival as
soon as they saw me. The prisoners declared that their lord
had been duly acquainted with my coming. through those
messengers I had sent him from Tenciz; that he would be glad
to see me, and would repair to the spot as soon as he knew of
my arrival. My men, moreover, informed me that they had
sent one of the prisoners in search of the lord, and of some
provisions, but had kept the other as hostage. They also
advised me that they had found plenty of cacao, but no
maize at all, although there was pretty good pasturage for
horses.

On my arrival at Acuculin, I immediately inquired whether
the lord of the place was come, or the messenger returned,
but I was told they had not come. I then addressed myself
to the other Indian prisoner, and asked him how it was that
his lord had not made his appearance. His answer was that
he was very much astonished at it, but could give no other

reason for his absence except his waiting until I personally
had arrived on the spot. That, now that he was aware of
my presence, he had no doubt he would come. I waited
two days, and seeing he did not arrive, I again applied to
the Indian, who said he knew well the spot where his lord
was, and that if I sent thither some of my Spaniards, he
would undertake to guide them, and deliver my message.
To this I agreed, and gave him ten Spaniards, whom he
conducted through a mountainous district to a place about
five leagues distant, where they found some huts. According to the report made by the Spaniards, the huts were
empty; but bore visible traces of having been recently inhabited. That very night the guide took flight, and the
Spaniards returned to the camp without accomplishing the
object for which I had sent them.

Seeing myself without a guide of any sort—through
which our difficulties were likely to be increased twofold—I
determined to send people in all directions, Spaniards as
well as Indians, to spread over that province, and see what
information they could gather and bring me. They marched
during eight consecutive days without meeting any living
creature, save some women, who were of little use for our
purpose, since they could neither shew us the road, nor tell
us about the lord of the land or his people. One of them,
however, said she knew of a village called Chianteco, about
two leagues further on, where I might find people able to
give me the information I required, and news of the Spaniards.
In the village, she added, resided many merchants, who
travelled to all parts with merchandise. I sent forthwith
some of my men, and gave them that woman for a guide;
but although the village was two good days' march through
a deserted country and bad roads, the natives had previous
notice of my coming, and not one of them could be secured
to act as guide on the occasion.

Our Almighty Lord, however, permitted that whilst we

were in a state of utmost despair, finding ourselves without
a guide, and unable to use the compass, in the midst of
mountains so intricate and rough that we had never seen
the like of them before, with no other practicable road but
the one on which we were, my men suddenly came upon a
lad of about fifteen years of age, who, being interrogated,
said he would guide us to certain habitations in Taniha,[1]
which was another of the provinces through which I recollected that I had to pass. As according to the lad's report the
habitations of Taniha were only two days' journey from the
place in which we then were, I hastily repaired thither, and
arrived two days after on the spot, when the out-runners of
my little host succeeded in securing an old Indian, who
guided us to the very villages of Taniha, situated two days'
march beyond. At this latter place four Indians were taken
prisoners, who, being interrogated by me, gave very positive
information about the Spaniards in search of whom I came,
declaring that they had actually seen them, and that they
were at a place called Nito,[2] distant only two days' march.
I immediately recollected that such was the name of the
place where, according to other reports, the Spaniards had
settled, and about which those merchants of Aculan had
spoken to me as being a town of great traffic and much re-
sorted to. In this opinion I was confirmed by the testimony
of two women, who said that at the time the Spaniards took
possession of the town they were residing in it; and as they
came by night and took the inhabitants unawares, they,
with other women, had been made prisoners and had
fallen to the lot of certain Christians, whom they designated
by their proper names, and in whose service they had remained for a length of time.

I cannot describe to your Majesty my joy, and that of all
my people, when the natives of Taniha gave us this news,

[1] Elsewhere Janiha.
[2] Now San Gil de Golfo Dulce.

seeing that we were so near the end of the perilous journey
we had undertaken. For, although the last four days'
march from Acuculin had been attended with great danger
and fatigue, owing to the precipitous roads and awful mountain passes we had to cross, it was nothing in comparison of
what we had suffered on the previous days. I have already
informed your Majesty that the few horses we had left
had been disabled by frequent falls among the rocks, and
that a cousin of mine, Juan de Avalos by name, had fallen,
he and his horse, down a precipice and broken his arm;[1] and
had it not been for the plates of the steel armour he
wore, which to a certain degree broke the violence of the
fall, he might have been dashed to pieces against the rocks·
I have told elsewhere how we extricated him from his position, and how we brought him up, and had to carry him over
those mountains, and the many tribulations and wants we had
to suffer during that perilous march, besides the extreme
hunger to which we had been reduced in the last days of our
adventurous peregrination. For, although there were still
some pigs left of those I brought from Mexico, when we
arrived at Taniha, neither I nor my men had tasted any
bread for eight consecutive days, our provision being entirely exhausted, our only food consisting of palmettos boiled
with the meat, and without salt, and the cores of the palm
trees. Nor was food more abundant in these villages of
Taniha; for being situated so close to the settlements of
the Spaniards, most of the inhabitants fearing a visit from
them, had fled elsewhere, although, had they known the
miserable plight in which I afterwards found my countrymen, they might have been secure against any inroad on their
part.

The happy news received at this place made us, however,
forget our past tribulations, and gave us courage to endure

[1] See above, p. 61, where it is clearly stated that "he broke his leg
in two or three places."

present miseries and troubles, especially that of hunger, against which we had to fight more resolutely than ever, for even those cores of palm-trees without salt, which, as I said before, constituted our principal aliment, could not be procured in sufficient quantity, for they had to be extracted from the stems of large and very high palm-trees, with such difficulty that two men had to work a whole day to procure that which they could eat in half-an-hour.

I was further told by those Indians who had given me news of the Spaniards, that before arriving at Nito I should have to march for two days over a bad road, and that close to the place there was a very large river, that could not be passed except in canoes, being so wide and the current so strong that it was impossible for us to swim across. Hearing this, I sent in that direction fifteen of my Spaniards on foot, and guided by one of those Indians, with orders to explore the roads and the river, and see if they could seize on one of those Spaniards, and ascertain from him to what party or division the settlers at Nito belonged, whether to those sent by me under Christoval de Olid and Francisco de las Casas, or to those who had followed the banners of Gil Gonzalez de Avila. The men started on their exploring expedition, and arrived, under the Indian's guidance, at a spot on the banks of the river, where they took possession of a canoe belonging to certain merchants of the place. Having hidden themselves inside, they lay in ambush until they saw coming from the opposite bank of the river a canoe with four Spaniards in it, who were fishing. These they seized upon, without letting any of them escape, or the people of the neighbouring village being aware of the fact; and, when brought before me, I interrogated them, and they informed me that the settlers in the neighbourhood belonged to the division of Gil Gonzalez de Avila, and that they were all sick and half-starved. Hearing this, I sent in that very canoe belonging to those Spaniards two servants of mine,

who were to be the bearers of a letter to the people of the
place, informing them of my arrival in those parts, and of
my intention to cross that river at that spot, for which purpose I begged very much that they should send me all the
canoes and boats they could dispose of. This being done,
and the messengers departed, I moved on slowly towards
the river side with the whole of my small army, which took
me three whole days. Soon after my arrival, I was visited
by one Diego Nieto, who said he was there under a sentence
of exile. He procured me a boat and a canoe, in which I
embarked with ten or twelve of my suite, crossing that very
night the river, although with great danger of being drowned,
for in the middle of the stream we were assailed by a gale
of wind, and as the river is there very wide, and the crossing
was effected very close to its mouth, we were on the point
of being lost. God our Lord was pleased, however, to preserve us on the occasion, and we reached the port in safety.
On the following day I fitted out another boat I found in the
harbour, by means of which, and of other boats and canoes procured in the vicinity, and which I caused to be well tied and
secured two by two, I managed to have the whole of my
small army, horses and luggage, on this side of the river, in
which operation no less than five or six days were spent.

The Spaniards whom I found settled in that place really
belonged to the expedition commanded by Gil Gonzalez de
Avila, and had been left there by him. They were eighty
in number, sixty men and twenty women. They were in
such a miserable plight that it really moved us to pity to see
them, and had I not arrived at that moment amongst them,
not one could have escaped; for, besides being few in number and having no weapons, they were all sick or wounded,
and almost starved to death. All the provision which they
brought from the island, and a little more that they had procured in the town when they first took it from the natives, was
long ago completely exhausted; neither had they the means

of procuring others, or overrunning the adjacent country, for
they were so situated in a sort of nook, without any issue by
land, that they could hardly stir out except by water, as we
afterwards found. I need scarcely say what their joy was
when they saw us arrive, looking upon us as their saviours,
and making all sorts of demonstrations.

Considering the extreme want in which those people were,
I immediately set about finding them means of support until
I could procure vessels to send them back to the island,
where they might supply their wants and recover their
strength; for, as I have said before, there were scarcely
eight men and women in the whole lot able to people the
land in case of their being left in that spot. I therefore
selected among my own men those who were to go in search
of provisions, and having fitted out two boats belonging to
the Spaniards of that place, and five or six canoes, which
I procured elsewhere, despatched them in various directions by sea. The first of these exploring parties I sent to
the mouth of a river called Yasa, about two leagues from the
settlement of the Spaniards, and in the direction of the territory through which I had come, having learned from the natives that the country around was well populated and full of
provisions. My men arrived at the river, and ascended it for
about six leagues, when they came upon some cultivated
fields of tolerable dimension; but the natives seeing them
approach, took up in haste all the food they had in certain
houses, and carrying away with them their sons and wives,
and all their valuables, fled to the mountains and hid themselves. It happened, however, that on the arrival of the
Spaniards at those houses, the rain began to fall heavily,
which obliged them to take shelter inside; and as they
were wet through they lighted fires, every one taking
off his armour and most of them their clothes to have them
dried. In this condition, and when they least thought, they
were suddenly assailed by the natives, who wounded most

of them in such a manner that they were obliged to take to their boats and return to me without bringing anything to eat. When I saw their wounds—some of which were considerable—I was exceedingly grieved, not only on account of the harm the men had sustained, but because they had done nothing towards alleviating our common troubles and wants, not to say anything of the confidence the Indians would take at seeing our discomfiture.

Immediately after this I sent, in the same boats and canoes, and under the command of one of my captains, another party of men, more numerous than the first, and composed of Spaniards as well as Mexicans. And finding that the boats and canoës would not hold all, I made some of them cross over the great river on which the village stood, ordering them to follow the river-side, whilst the boats and canoes went close to the shore and in sight of it, in order to take them over other streams and bays, of which there seemed to be many. In this manner they came up to the mouth of that large river, and to the spot where, on a former occasion, my Spaniards had been surprised and wounded; but without proceeding any further on their exploration, they returned to me without executing my orders or bringing any provision, although they took possession of one canoe and four Indians. Being asked why they came back in that way empty-handed, they answered that, owing to the great rains, the river had so swollen and the current was so strong, that they had not been able to ascend it for more than a league. That they had waited in vain during eight consecutive days for the waters of the river to go down, but having no provisions or fire with them, and indeed no other food but the fruit of wild trees, they had been obliged to return. These men were true in their report, for they were so worn out by fatigue, and so debilitated by hunger, that we had the greatest difficulty in restoring them to their former condition.

Great was my concern when I saw these two attempts

fail ; and had it not been for a few pigs that we had still remaining, and on which we went on feeding with the greatest
parsimony, without either bread or salt, we might all have
perished through hunger.   In this emergency I sent for the
four Indians that had been taken in the canoe, and asked
them through the interpreter if they knew of any place in
the neighbourhood where provisions might be procured,
promising that if they guided me to it I would set them at
liberty and make them presents of many things.   One of
them then answered that he was a merchant, and that the
other three men were his servants; that he often visited
that coast with his ships, and that he knew of a certain gulf
leading to a great river, where in winter time and when the
sea was stormy all the merchants like himself navigated, and
that on the banks of that river there were considerable villages, inhabited by rich people and well stocked with all
manner of provisions, and that he would conduct me or my
people to certain habitations where I might find everything
I could wish for.   He further said that in order to prove to
me that his statement was correct, he consented to be put in
chains, and if he told a lie, to be punished as he deserved.
I again gave orders that the boats and canoes should be prepared, and having placed in them all the men of my company[1] who were still healthy and capable of bearing fatigue,
sent them under the guidance of that man ; but ten days
afterwards they came back just as they had departed, saying
that the guide had conducted them to certain morasses,
where neither boats nor canoes could float, and which they
could not pass notwithstanding all their efforts.   Having
then asked the guide how it came to be that with all his
protestations I had been deceived, he answered me that
what he said was the exact truth, and that it was no fault of
his if the Spaniards I had sent along with him would not go

[1] Cortes seems to have divided his Spaniards into companies, and to
have himself taken the command of one.

on, as he recommended them to do; they had been very
close to the spot where the river joined the sea, and some of
them even owned that they had heard the distant murmur
of the waves.

I cannot express the feelings of horror and dismay that
assailed me when I saw my hopes thus baffled for the third
time, and calculated that not one of us could possibly escape
death by starvation. But in this state of mind, and not
knowing what to do, God Almighty, who in such extreme
emergencies is always at hand, showing His favours to those
persons who least deserve them, as myself, no doubt because
I am employed in your Majesty's service, was pleased to
bring us help and assistance whence we did least expect it.
For there happened to arrive in those very days a vessel
from the islands with thirty men, exclusive of the crew,
thirteen horses, seventy and odd pigs, besides twelve casks
of salted meat, and thirteen loads of bread of the kind used
in the islands.[1] We all most earnestly thanked our God
for the timely succour thus received, and having treated
with the master, bought of him all those provisions, besides
the vessel herself, for the sum of 4,000 dollars.

Some time previous to the arrival of those Spaniards, I
had set about repairing a caravel which the people of that
village had almost allowed to rot, and to build, with the
pieces of other vessels that lay scattered here and there on
the shore, a good-sized brigantine. When, therefore, this
vessel from the islands arrived so unexpectedly among us,
the caravel was completely finished and ready to take the
sea; but I do believe that the brigantine's work could never
have been done, had not a man come in that vessel's crew
who, although not a carpenter himself, knew enough of that
craft to help us in our work.

Some time after this, having sent parties of men in all
directions by land, a path was discovered across mountains,

---

[1] That called *cazabe*.

distant eighteen leagues from the place where I then was, and leading to some habitations where plenty of food was found, though, owing to the great distance and bad roads, it was of little or no avail. At these habitations, known by the name of Leguela,[1] some Indians were taken, who told us that the place where Francisco de las Casas, and Christoval de Olid, and Gil Gonzalez de Avila had resided, and whereat the said Christoval de Olid died, was a town called Naco, as I have already informed your Majesty, and wil again hereafter. The same statement had been made to me by the Spaniards I found at Nito,[2] and therefore I gave orders to clear the road, and sent forward all my men, foot and horse, under one of my captains, keeping only with me the servants of my household, the sick and invalids, and a few more who preferred going by sea. I gave my instructions to that captain and bade him repair to the said town of Naco, and try to pacify the inhabitants of the province, who, in consequence of the arrival of those Spaniards among them, were rather excited and disturbed. When at Naco, he was to send ten or twelve horsemen and as many crossbowmen to the bay and port of Saint Andrew, which is about twenty leagues from that place. In the meantime, I, with the sick and wounded, and the rest of the army, would proceed thither by sea, and wait for them in case I arrived first; if, on the contrary, they were on the spot before me, they were to encamp and wait for orders.

[1] All copies present the same reading, and therefore there can be no doubt as to the name of this place, which is not on the maps.

[2] The Vienna MS. has: "Tambien de ello tuve yo noticia por aquellos españoles que hallé en aquel pueblo de Leguela;" but this is evidently an error, which originated no doubt in Cortes' secretary writing *Leguela* instead of *Nito*. It was at this latter place, and not at Leguola, that the conqueror of Mexico met with the Spaniards. See above, p. 68. Nito and Naco, though frequently confounded by ancient and modern writers, are two distinct places. The former has since lost its name, and is now known as San Gil de Buena Vista, on the Golfo Dulce. Naco is the name of a pleasant and spacious valley, surrounded by fertile hills, between San Pedro Zula and Puerto Caballos.

The people gone, and the brigantine being made fit for sea, I thought of embarking in her and in the other vessels with the remainder of my people; but I found that, although we had salt meat enough, we had not sufficient bread, and that it was a very adventurous thing to put to sea without this article, especially with so many sick people as I had on board, for were we to encounter bad weather or contrary winds, we were sure to die of hunger, instead of finding remedy for our wants. But, whilst I was considering what could best be done in such an emergency, the master of that vessel that came from the islands, and was bought by me, as I have already informed your Majesty, called upon me and said that he himself had formed part of the expedition of Gil Gonzalez when he came to those parts; that he had two hundred men, one good brigantine, and four other vessels; and that, with the said brigantine and the boats of the vessels, they had gone a good way up that river, and met with two great gulfs, the waters of which were sweet; and that all around those two gulfs there were several villages, well stocked with food. That they had navigated to the very end of them, for a distance of fourteen leagues up the river, when all of a sudden the stream became so narrow and at the same time so impetuous and strong, that in six days they could only make four leagues, notwithstanding the waters were still very deep. That owing to that circumstance they had been unable to ascertain where the river led to; but that he believed it led to a country abounding in maize. "But," he added, "you have not men enough to go on such a voyage of exploration; for when we were on that river, eighty of us landed and entered a certain village without being seen, but soon after the natives returned in such force, and attacked us with such fury, that we had to take to our ships, and some of us were wounded.

Seeing, however, the extreme want in which my men were, and that it was far preferable to cross the land in

search of food, however perilous the route might be, than
to expose myself to the dangers of the sea without sufficient
provisions, I determined at once to go up that river; for,
besides finding food for the people under me—which was
then my principal care—it struck me that I might make
some discovery whereby to be of service to your Majesty. I
immediately mustered the force I had with me, that is, those
who were still able to bear the fatigues of a march, and I
found it to consist of only forty Spaniards, who, though not
sufficiently strong for every kind of work, were nevertheless
well enough to remain in guard of the ships whenever I
might choose to land. With these forty Spaniards, and
about fifty Indians[1] who still remained out of those I brought
from Mexico, I went on board the said brigantine, already
fit for sea, and with two other boats and four canoes set out
in the direction of that river that we were to ascend, leaving
inland all my sick people and a steward of mine to attend
to them and provide them with food. Our navigation up
the river was at first very hard and troublesome, owing to
the strength of the current; but after two nights and one
day we came to the first of the two gulfs above alluded to,
a distance of about three leagues from the place of our starting. The gulf may measure about twelve leagues round,
but its shores are completely deserted, being very low and
swampy. We navigated its waters during twenty-four hours,
until we came to a sort of narrow bay made by the river,
into which I penetrated, and on the following day arrived
at the other gulf, which is certainly one of the finest things
to behold, for in the midst of a rocky and precipitous chain
of mountains there was a magnificent bay, which could very
well measure thirty leagues round. I followed close inland,
until perceiving near the shore a village, and a path leading

---

[1] *Cincuenta* in all the copies; but it is hardly to be believed that so
large a number should have perished on the road, Cortes himself stating
elsewhere that they exceeded three thousand.

to it, I landed, and at about two-thirds of a league, came
upon some houses, the inhabitants of which had no doubt
seen us in the distance; for they were deserted and completely emptied. We found, however, in the neighbouring
fields abundance of green maize, of which we ate that night
and the morning of the following day; but as we did not
find there what we wanted, we made provision of that green
maize, and returned to our boats, without meeting with any
of the natives. In sailing across the gulf, which was
effected with some difficulty, owing to a strong contrary
wind that overtook us in the middle of it, one of the canoes
was overset; but the people in her were saved by the crew
of one of the boats, except one Indian, who was drowned.
It was late in the evening when we touched the shore, but
could not land until the following morning; when entering
a small stream that emptied its waters at that spot, and
leaving the brigantine behind, I began to explore it with
the boats and canoes. In this manner I came to a place on
the shore where there appeared to be a pathway, and having
given orders that the boats and canoes should return to the
gulf by the brigantine's side, I landed with thirty of my
men and all the Indians, and, following the pathway, came
at about a quarter of a league upon a village, which seemed
to have been abandoned by its inhabitants many days before,
for the houses were full of weeds, although there was in the
vicinity many a fine orchard filled with cacao and other
fruit-trees. I went round the village to see if there was a
road, and found one at last, but it was so rough that it
seemed as if it had not been trod for some time. However,
finding no other, I determined to follow that one, and we
marched on that day five leagues, over mountains so rugged
and steep, that we had to make use of our hands and feet in
climbing. We then came to some maize plantations, where,
in a house standing in the middle of them, we took three
women and a man, to whom, no doubt, these fields belonged.

By these women we were guided to other plantations, where
we took two more women, and thence to a large tract of
cultivated land, and in the centre of it about forty houses,
very small, but newly built.   It would appear, however,
that the people had been informed of our arrival, for when
we came the village was deserted, and the inhabitants had
fled to the mountains. . But as we came upon them so suddenly, they could not carry away all their property, and left
behind many things, principally fowls, pigeons, partridges,
and pheasants, which they kept in cages.   There was, however, no dried maize, and no salt.   We passed the night at
this place, and somewhat relieved our wants, having satisfied
our hunger with the fowls and some green maize which
we found in the plantations.

We had been in that village more than two hours, when
two of the natives, unconscious of having such guests, returned to their houses, and were taken prisoners by the
sentries I had placed at the entrance.   Being asked by me
whether they knew of any other village in the vicinity, they
answered that there was one, and that they would willingly
conduct me to it on the next day, though, the distance
being considerable, we could only reach it late in the evening, and almost by night.   On the following morning, therefore, we undertook our march, guided by those two Indians,
by roads still worse than those of the previous day; for,
besides their being quite as covered with low wood and
brambles, we had at every arrow's throw to cross some
river of the many that empty their waters in the gulf.   For
it is owing to the great accumulation of waters that come
down from the mountains that those gulfs and lagoons are
formed, and that the river I have described to your Majesty
flows with such rapidity and force.   Thus, without meeting
any habitations, and crossing no less than five-and-forty of
those large streams, not including in that number several
rivulets, we made about seven leagues of that bad road.

Whilst we were marching under the guidance of those men, we met three Indian women loaded with maize, and coming from that very village whither we were being conducted; and having asked them whether the report of our guides was a true one, they certified us of it. At sunset of that same day we heard a sound as of beating drums, and having asked the women what it could be, they said that it was a festival in the village. As, whenever I came to one, I did my utmost to take the inhabitants by surprise, on this occasion I took every precaution not to be seen. I hid my people, as well as I could, in the crevices of the mountain, and placed sentries almost above the village, and on the road, with orders to secure any Indian that might make his appearance at that hour. I thus passed the night on that mountain, but it rained so hard all the time, and we were so pestered by mosquitos, that we could not remain where we were. Two or three times during the night we attempted to come down from the mountain, and assail the village; but it was so dark and stormy, that although the village was close by, and we could almost hear the natives speak to each other, we never succeeded in finding our way to it. We waited, therefore, until daybreak, when we came down with such opportunity, that we took them all in their sleep. I had given positive orders that nobody should enter a private dwelling, or shout, or utter war-cries, but enjoined them, on the contrary, to surround in silence the largest and best-looking houses, specially that of the chief, and one resembling a great barrack, where we had been told that all the warriors of the place congregated together. These precautions being taken, God permitted that the first building we came to was that where the warriors were assembled. It was already daylight, and as one of my men saw so many people armed, and considered how few in number we were to attack them with success, although asleep, he began to shout our usual war-cry, saying "Santiago, Santiago!"

At this rumour and noise the Indians woke, when some
of them took to their weapons and others did not; but the
house having no walls, and the roof being supported only
by wooden posts, most of the Indians, on our entering the
place, fled in every direction, especially as it was too large
to be completely surrounded.

I can assure your Highness that if that Spaniard had not,
contrary to my orders, begun to shout in the manner he did,
I should have taken every one of them prisoners, and it
might have turned out the finest feat of arms ever made
in those parts, and been the cause of the pacification of all
the land. For after explaining the reason of my coming
among them, and promising to do them no injury, I would
have set them free; and they, seeing the manner in which
they were treated, and that I meant no harm, would un-
doubtedly have become my friends, instead of bitter enemies,
as they afterwards proved to be. This notwithstanding, we
took in the village fifteen men and twenty women, besides
ten or twelve men more, who chose death rather than
to be taken alive, and among these their chief, whose
body was afterwards identified and shown to me by the
prisoners themselves. Nor did we find at this village anything that could be of use to supply our wants, for although
there was plenty of green maize in the fields, it was not the
sort of food that we came in search of.

In this village I remained two days, with a view to afford
some rest to my people. Having asked the Indians made
prisoners at the place whether they knew of any other village in the vicinity where dried maize could be obtained,
they answered me that they knew of one, called Chacujal,[1]
a very populous and ancient one, where all manner of provisions might be found in abundance. With this information I set on, guided by those Indians, in the direction of

---

[1] Only one of the copies affords this reading, which seems to me the
most acceptable; all others having Chaantel, Chuantel, or Chuhantel.

the village described ; and having marched during that day
six long leagues of bad road cut by many a river, arrived at
some extensive plantations, which our guides told us belonged to the village in question. Following, then, for
about two leagues a mountain path in sight of the said cultivated fields, and using every precaution not to be felt or
seen by the natives, we came upon a troop of eight Indians,
who, not knowing who we were, came to meet us, and were
taken prisoners by my scouts and people in the van. They
were all either labourers who had gone out to cut wood, or
hunters. At about sunset I was told by the guides to halt,
as the village was close by. I did as they told me, and
passed three hours of the night hid in a forest, after which
I began to march, still guided by those Indians, until we
came to a river, which we crossed with the water up to our
breasts, though the current was so strong that, had we not
taken the precaution of holding each other by the hand,
some of us might have been carried away by the force of it.
The river once crossed in the manner just explained, and
the guides having again told me that the village was close
at hand, I ordered the men to halt, and went myself with
two companies to see if the report was true. Proceeding
without noise, I came to a spot whence I could distinctly
see the houses, and even hear the voices of the people inside ; everything seemed quiet, and the natives unconscious
of our arrival. I then returned to my own people, leaving
on each side of the road that led to the village six men to
keep watch and inform me of what they saw. I had laid
down on some straw, in order to rest, when one of the
scouts came to me, and said that by the road communicating
with the village he saw a body of armed men coming down
upon us ; but that they marched without any order or precaution, speaking to each other, and as if they were ignorant
of our being on their passage. I immediately summoned my
men up, and made them arm themselves as quickly and

noiselessly as they could; but as the distance between the
village and the place where we had encamped was so short,
before we were ready to meet them the Indians discovered
the scouts, and letting fly on them a volley of their arrows,
began to retreat towards their village, fighting all the time
with those of my men who were foremost.   In this manner
we entered the village mixed up with them; but the night
being dark, the Indians suddenly disappeared in the streets,
and we could find no enemies.   Fearing some ambush, and
suspecting that the people of the village had been somehow
informed of our arrival, I gave orders to my men to keep
well together, and marching through the place, arrived at a
great square, where they had their mosques and houses of
worship; and as we saw the mosques and the buildings
round them just in the manner and form of those of Culúa,
we were more overawed and astonished than we had been
hitherto, since nowhere since we left Aculan had we seen
such signs of policy and power.   There were even some
among us who expressed the opinion that we ought immediately to return and cross the river that very night, before
the people of the village, perceiving how few we were, took
possession of that pass, and cut from us all retreat.   The advice
was not bad, considering what we had already seen of the
place, and what we could expect from its inhabitants; but it
seemed to me that we could not depart in that way, for if we
did, the enemy would be made aware sooner of our weak-
ness, and therefore attack us in our retreat, whereas by remaining where we were, we gave signs of courage, by which
the Indians might be overawed.   And so it happened, for
after remaining in that large square for a length of time
without being molested in the least, or hearing any noise
whatever, I entered with my men one of those spacious halls
which they generally have near the temples of their idols,
and soon after sent out some of my men to report what they
saw or heard in the village.   They soon came back to me,

full of joy, saying that not only had they not heard any one
stir in the village, but that the houses had all been deserted by their inmates, and that in every one of them
there was fire burning, and a good stock of provisions. We,
however, passed that night on watch, and on the following
morning sent out several parties of men to explore the village, which was well designed, the houses well built, and
close to each other. We found in them plenty of cotton,
woven or raw, much linen of Indian manufacture, and of
the best kind, great quantities of dried maize, cacao, beans,
peppers and salt, many fowls, and pheasants in cages, partridges, and dogs of the species they keep for eating, and which
are very tasteful to the palate, and in short every variety of
food in such abundance, that had our ship and boats been
near at hand, we might easily have loaded enough of it to
last us for many a day; but unfortunately we were twenty
leagues off, had no means of carrying provisions except on
the backs of men, and we were all of us in such a condition
that, had we not refreshed ourselves a little at that place,
and rested for some days, I doubt much whether we should
have been able to return to our boats. On the next day I
sent for one of the natives of the place, who, as I have said
before, had been taken prisoner in the plantations, and
seemed to be a person of some importance, for he was taken
with his bow and arrows hunting, and was very well dressed
according to the manner of the Indians; and having spoken
to him through an interpreter, bade him go to the chief of
the village and its inhabitants, and tell them in my name
that I was not come among them for the purpose of causing
annoyance, but merely to entertain them on matters which
concerned them much. That if the lord of the place or
some of the chief inhabitants came to see me, they would
learn the cause of my coming, and be sure that if they came
much good would result to them; and on the contrary, if
they refused, they might suffer from it. I therefore de-

spatched that Indian with a letter[1] of mine to the chief of
the village, having found by experience that my letters
had always the effect of inspiring confidence in the people
of those parts.   But I must confess that I did it against the
advice of some of my people, who said it was imprudent to
send the Indian with such a message, because he could not
fail to inform his countrymen of the smallness of our number.   That the village was large and populous, as it appeared from the quantity of houses built close together.
That the inhabitants, seeing how few we were, might easily
send to their neighbours for assistance, and fall at once upon
us.   The advice was good ; yet, wishing to find the means
of effectually provisioning my little army, and believing that
if those people came to me with peaceable intentions they
might perhaps suggest the manner of carrying away some of
the food we had collected, I decided to sacrifice everything
to that important object ; for in truth there was no less danger for us in quitting the place without a stock of provisions
for the future, than in fighting with those Indians, in case
they might have come down upon us.   All these considera-
tions decided me to despatch the Indian, as I did, he promising to return on the following day, as he said he knew
the spot where the chief man of the place and his people
might be.

On the day after this, which was that appointed for the
return of the Indian, as two of my Spaniards were making
the round of the village, and exploring the fields in the
neighbourhood, they found the letter I had given the
messenger stuck upon a pole by the side of the road, whence
I concluded that I should never get an answer to it.   And

---

[1] *Y así le despaché con una carta mia*, which leaves no doubt whatever as to the meaning ; and yet one would feel inclined to inquire how
the people of Guatemala and Honduras could be made to understand
the Mexican hieroglyphics, for it is not to be supposed that the letter
was in Spanish.

so it was, for the Indian messenger never returned; and, although we remained full eighteen days at that place, resting and considering about the means of carrying away some of the provisions found at the houses, never in all that time did we cast our eye on a living creature.

One day the idea struck me that by following down the river of that village I might perhaps come to the other large river that empties itself in the sweet gulfs, where I had left my brigantine, as well as my boats and canoes. I consulted the matter with some of the prisoners of that village, and they all seemed to agree in saying that the two rivers communicated; but as they did not understand us well, and they spoke a language totally different from those we had hitherto met, no great reliance could be placed in their information. Through signs, however, and aided by a few words in that language which I understood, I begged that two of them should accompany ten of my Spaniards, and show them the meeting of the two rivers. This they promised to do, adding that the place was near at hand, and that they would be back on the next day. And so it was, for God permitted that after marching two leagues through very fine orchards, full of cacao and other fruit trees, they should guide my men to the banks of that large river, which they said communicated with the gulf, where my shipping was. They even went so far as to say that the river's name was Apolochic, and that they had often navigated it. On their return, the next day, I asked them how many days it would take a canoe to go down the river to the gulfs, and having answered me that five days were sufficient to accomplish the journey, I determined upon sending thither two Spaniards, accompanied by one of the guides, who offered to take them by cross-roads known to him to the very spot on the gulf where my ships were. I gave my men instructions to have the brigantine, boats and canoes taken to the mouth of that large river, and that, leaving the vessel behind, they should

try with one of the canoes and a boat to ascend the river to
the spot where the other one joined it. This being done,
and the men despatched on their errand, I ordered four
rafters to be constructed with pieces of timber and very
large bamboos, capable of supporting forty faneagues or
bushels of dried maize and ten men each, without counting
a quantity of beans, peppers and cacao, which each Spaniard
afterwards threw into it for his own private supply. The
rafters being made, after eight days' hard work, and the
provisions placed on them, the Spaniards I had sent to the
brigantine came to me and said that, after ascending the
river during six consecutive days, they had found it impossible for the boat to go on, and had left it behind with
ten Spaniards to guard it; that prosecuting their journey
with the canoe, they had arrived at a place, about one league
down the river, where, worn out by fatigue, and unable to
use their oars, they had left it hidden among the bushes.
That on their way up the river they had met Indians, and
fought occasionally with them, and although they were then
few in number, they had reason to fear that they would
come back in force, and wait for their return. I immediately sent people to look out for the canoe, and bring it along-
side of the rafters; and having placed on these all the provisions we had collected, chose among my people those who
were most capable of directing those rafts, and avoiding
by means of great poles the many floating timbers and
gigantic trees with which the bed of the river was covered,
and which rendered the navigation extremely dangerous.
The remainder of my people, under a captain appointed for
the purpose, I sent to the gulf by the same route which we
had followed in coming up to Chacujal,[1] with instructions
that if they arrived before me they were to wait at the
place of our landing until I should come for them, and that
if, on the contrary, I was before them on the spot, I would

[1] The same place mentioned at page 82.

not move until they came. As to myself, I embarked in
the canoe with only two crossbow-men, the only ones dis-
posable in all my suite. Though the journey I was about
to undertake was exceedingly dangerous, owing to the im-
petuosity and strength of the current, as well as the almost
certainty that the Indians would wait for us on our passage,
I nevertheless preferred this route by water to the other by
water, because our stock of provisions went this way, and I
could thus watch better over it. And so, trusting myself in
the hands of God, our Saviour, I began descending the
river with such rapidity, owing to the strength and violence
of the current, that in less than three hours' navigation we
came to the spot where the boat had been left. Here we
attempted to lighten the rafts by putting part of their
cargo in the boat, but it was found impracticable, for no
human effort could stop the rafts, driven on as they were
by a rapid current. I then embarked in the boat, and gave
orders that the canoe, well fitted with good oars, should go
in front of the rafts, in order to see whether any Indians
lay in ambush, or whether we came to any dangerous pass
in the river; I myself remaining behind with the boat ready
to give assistance to the rafts, as it was clear to me that, in
case of need, I might more easily help from the rear than
if placed in the van. In this order we went down that river,
until about sunset, when one of the rafts struck violently
against a piece of timber that held fast to the bottom. So
strong was the shock, that the raft was almost entirely
submerged, and although the violence of the waters at that
spot made it float again, half its cargo was lost. Three
hours later in the night, I heard in front of us the shouting
of some Indians, but not choosing to leave the rafts behind,
I did not go forward to ascertain what it might be. The
snouting, however, ceased, and we heard no more of it for
some time. A little later in the night I again heard the
shouts, at what seemed to me a shorter distance; but I could

not ascertain the fact, for the canoe went, as I have said, in front, then came three of the rafts, and I followed in the rear with the fourth, which, owing to the accident sustained, could not go so fast.

In this manner we proceeded for some length of time, until we came to a turning of the river, where the current was so strong that, notwithstanding all our efforts, rafts and boat were cast on shore. Some time before this, hearing no longer those alarming shouts, confidence had returned to my people, and I myself, taking off my helmet—for I was ill with fever at the time—had laid my head on my hand to see if I could rest. It was soon, however, ascertained that the shouting we had heard in the distance came from that particular spot, for the Indians, who knew the river well, as inhabiting its banks, and being almost born on it, had followed us for some time along the shore, knowing very well that we should be cast by the current on the very spot where they were waiting in ambush for us. No sooner, therefore, did the canoe and rafts reach the place where the Indians lay concealed, than we were assailed by a volley of arrows from the shore, that wounded almost every man on board ; though, knowing that most of us remained still behind, the attack of the Indians was by no means so strong or furious as the one they afterwards made on us. Thus assailed, the people in the canoe attempted to come back, and give me notice of the danger ; but they never succeeded in porting the helm, owing to the strength of the current. When, however, it came to our turn to strike the land, the Indians gave a most terrific shout, and assailed us with such a volley of arrows and stones, that not one man on board escaped without a wound. I myself was struck by a stone on the head, the only part of my body that was unarmed, having taken off my steel cap some time before. God, however, permitted that at the spot where this happened, the banks of the river should be high, and the waters deep. To this circumstance we owed our salvation; for the night being dark, some of the Indians who attempted to leap upon the rafts and boat, fell into the water, and I believe that a good number of them were drowned in this way. The current itself soon extricated us from the danger, so that a few minutes after this we scarcely heard their shouts.

The rest of the night passed without encounter of any sort, though from time to time we still heard in the distance, or from the sides of the river, the Indian war-cries. The shores, I observed, were covered with villages and plantations, and there were, besides, very fine orchards with cacao and other fruit trees.

At dawn of day we were five leagues from the mouth of that river that empties itself into the gulf, and where the brigantine was waiting for us, and about the hour of noon we arrived on the spot, so that in four-and-twenty hours we ran no less than twenty long leagues down that river.

Having given orders that the provisions on the rafts should be transferred immediately to the brigantine, I was informed, to my great disappointment, that most of the maize was wet, and that if I could not have it dried, I ran a risk of losing the whole stock, whereby all the trouble we had in procuring it would have proved in vain. I immediately caused the dry maize to be put aside and stored in the brigantine; and as to that which had been spoilt by water, I had it thrown into the two boats and in two canoes, and sent in haste to the village for the purpose of drying; the shores of that gulf being so swampy and low that there was no spot, however small, where the operation could be effectually carried on. My men, therefore, went away with the boats and canoes, but I gave them orders to send the same back to me, the brigantine and one remaining canoe being insufficient to convey all my people. Soon after their departure I set sail in the brigantine, and steered towards the place where

it was agreed that I should wait for the people coming from
Chacujal by land. I waited for them three days, at the end
of which they all arrived in good spirits, and with no other
loss but that of a Spaniard, who having eaten of some herbs
he saw in the fields, died almost immediately after. They
also brought with them an Indian, whom they had surprised
and taken prisoner near the place where I left them. This
Indian was dressed differently and spoke a language unknown in these parts. I had already begun to interrogate
him by signs, when a man was found among the prisoners
who said he understood a little of his dialect. In this manner we learned that he was a native of Teculutlan. No
sooner did I hear that name pronounced, than I recollected having heard it repeated on other occasions, and
when I returned to the village I consulted certain memoranda
of mine, where I actually found that name written as being
that of a place across the country, between which and the
Spanish establishments in the South Sea, governed by Pedro
de Alvarado, one of my captains, there was only a distance of
seventy-eight leagues. The above memoranda further
stated that the village of Teculutlan had been visited by
Spaniards, and as the Indian bore also testimony to the fact,
I was very much pleased at receiving such intelligence.

My people being all congregated together, and the boats
not having yet returned, we consumed all the dry grain we
had in store, and embarked on board the brigantine, though
the vessel being so very small, we had the greatest difficulty to move. It was my idea to cross the gulf to
that village where we had landed at first, because I recollected that the maize plantations were very fine and in full
grain, though not sufficiently ripe for our cutting. Five-
and-twenty days had elapsed since that time, and it was to
be hoped that a good deal of it was dry enough for us to keep ;
and it so happened ; for being one morning in the middle
of the gulf, we saw the boats and canoes coming towards us,

and having sailed altogether in that direction, recognised
the place where the village was.   Immediately after landing, all my people, Spaniards as well as Indians, besides
forty native prisoners, went straight forward to the village,
where they found several maize plantations in the finest
possible condition.   The natives, if there were any at the
place, not having shown themselves or made any opposition,
my men reaped as much of that maize as they could, every
man of us, Christian or Indian, making that day three
journeys, fortunately very short, from the village to the
ship, loaded with as much grain as he could carry.   The
brigantine being filled as well as the boats, I went to
the village myself, leaving there all my people engaged in
that most providential harvest; I afterwards sent to them
the two boats, and one more belonging to a vessel from
New Spain, that had been lost in those waters, and four
canoes.   In these vessels all my people embarked, after
having, as I said before, brought sufficient provision to last
us all for many a day.   It was, indeed, a most providential
supply, and one that compensated us for all our past
troubles; for had we not found it at that moment, we should
all have perished through hunger.

Our provisions being safely stowed in the ship and boats,
I embarked with all the people of the division of Gil Gon-
ralez Leutville who were in that village,[1] and those who
still remained of my former army, and this being done, I set
sail on the   day of   ,[2] and steered for the
harbour in the bay of St. Andrew.[3]   I anchored near a point
of land, where having first landed all those who could make

---

[1] As the name of this village on the Golfo Dulce is nowhere given, I
am at a loss to determine whether Nito or San Gil is meant.   I rather
think it is a different place.

[2] None of the copies I have consulted gives the date of Cortes' departure for the bay of Honduras.

[3] San Andres, now called Puerto Caballos.

use of their legs, besides two horses that I had with me in
the ship, ordered them to march to the said harbour and
bay, where the people of Naco were to be already waiting
our arrival. My object in doing so was to lighten a little
the ship and boats, which, owing to their great cargoes, and
to the number of men stowed in them, sank rather too much
in the water, making the navigation at once difficult and
perilous. The road to Naco by land was, moreover, known
to us—as we had already passed it on a former occasion—
and afforded no difficulty, save certain streams of water
that had to be crossed, and on account of which I sent
along with them, close to the shore, a boat to help in the
crossing. On my arrival at the harbour, I found that the
people of Naco had preceded me by two days. I learned
from them that all the rest of the people were in good
health, and that they were abundantly provided with maize,
peppers, and other fruits of the land, but meat or salt they
had not, and for two months before they had tasted none.

I stayed there twenty days, seeing to what those settlers from
Naco had better do, and looking for a convenient spot to
found a city; for certainly that port is the best and the
largest that can be found in all that coast of Tierra Firme,
that is to say, from the Gulf of Pearls to Florida. God
permitted that I should find one very good for all purposes;
for having sent people to search the beds of some small rivers
in the neighbourhood, they returned to me with good
samples of fine gold discovered one or two leagues from
the spot which I had designated for a town. Owing to this
latter circumstance, and to the goodness of the harbour, and
to the fertile and populous districts in the neighbourhood,
it seemed to me that your majesty would be pleased to have
a town in this particular spot; and, therefore, I sent a
message to Naco, where the people [of Gil Gonzales] were
for the most part settled, to inquire whether any of them
would like to establish themselves there. As the land was

good, there were about fifty—most of them belonging to the
set that had come thither in my company—who consented to
change residence. And so, in your majesty's name, I founded
there a town, which I called the "Nativity of our Lady,"[1]
because on that very day the levelling of the ground com-
menced. I appointed alcaldes and municipal officers,[2] and
left with them clergymen, church ornaments, and all
necessaries for the celebration of the mass. I also left with
them workmen and mechanics, such as a smith, with a very
good forge and all the appendages of it, a carpenter and a
shipwright, a barber and a tailor. Among the settlers there
were twenty who possessed horses, and some who had crossbows. In fine, I provided them with a certain quantity of
powder and artillery. When, on my arrival at the place, I
heard from the people who had lately come from Naco that
the inhabitants of that village,[3] and others in the vicinity,
had deserted their dwellings and fled to the mountains, and
that they refused to return, though frequently invited to do
so, recollecting the injuries and bad treatment received at
the hands of Gil Gonzales, Christoval de Olid, and their
followers, I took immediate measures to stop the evil, and
gain, if possible, the confidence of the natives. I therefore
wrote to the captain who there governed in my name, to
try every means in his power to secure some of those
Indians and send them under an escort to me, that I might
speak to them and give every assurance that they should
not be in the least molested. The captain did as I told him,
and sent me a few Indians taken in a foray he had made for
the purpose, and whom I entertained and treated as well as
I could, speaking to them myself by means of an interpreter,

[1] La Natividad de Nuestra Señora.

[2] The Spanish word used is *regidores*, which cannot possibly be translated otherwise.

[3] The port of Saint Andrew (San Andres), where the new town,
Natividad, was founded.

or through some of the principal Mexicans I had with me.
They told them who I was, and what I had done in their
country, and how well they all had been treated by me since
they became my friends, and how they were protected and
governed in justice in everything concerning themselves,
their wives, their children, and their property; how, on the
contrary, those who were rebellious to your Majesty's authority I considered my enemies, and treated them as such,
doing them all the harm I could. These and other similar
suggestions had the effect of somewhat calming the fears of
the natives, who came to me saying, that they had well
understood what these Mexicans told them; but that they
still doubted of its being true, because those captains who
had arrived in their country before me had held a similar
language to them, and yet had told a lie; for immediately
after their submission, they had taken from them their wives
to make their bread, and the men to carry loads on their
backs; that they very much feared that notwithstanding my
promises I would do the same. I again spoke to them through
the interpreter, and through those Mexicans who came with
me, assuring them that what I told them was the plain truth;
and as they saw that the Indians of my suite seemed happy
and well treated, they had confidence in my words, and
went away promising to persuade their chiefs and comrades.
And so they did; for a few days after this, I received intelligence from the captain, saying that many Indian families
belonging to the neighbouring villages, such as Naco—where
the Spaniards had settled—Quimistlan, Zula, Cholome,[1] and
others, the smallest of which counted at least two thousand
houses or fires, had peaceably returned to their dwellings,
announcing that all the natives of that extensive province
would soon do the same, having been informed who I was,

---

[1] One of the copies has these names differently: Quimotlan, Zecla y
Tholoma; another one reads Zola y Choleme, whilst a third offers
Quimixtitlan.

and what my object was in coming among them, and other
things to that purpose which those Mexicans had told them.
They ended by a prayer that I should, as soon as possible,
visit them, for they were certain that with my coming all
the neighbouring provinces would make their submission.
This I would willingly have done, had I not been obliged
to proceed further on my march, in order to provide for
certain matters, about which I will say something to your
Majesty in the following chapter.

On my arrival, invincible Cæsar, at that village of Nito,
where, as I said before, I found the people of Gil Gonzalez
almost entirely forgotten and lost, I learned from them that
Francisco de las Casas, one of my lieutenants, whom I had
sent to inquire about Christoval de Olid and his men, and
to know what had become of them, had left at about sixty
leagues lower down the coast, in a harbour called by the
pilots Las Honduras, a certain number of Spaniards, who no
doubt were still there. No sooner, therefore, did I arrive at
that village of Saint Andrew (where, in your Majesty's name,
the town called Natividad de Nuestra Señora has since been
founded), than I began to consider which would be the best
means of communicating with them; and so, whilst I attended
to the said foundation and population, and gave my instructions to the captain and people at Naco as to what they were
to do for the pacification of the Indians in the neighbourhood,
I occupied myself about those people of Francisco de las Casas,
sending thither, to Honduras, the vessel I had bought, with
orders to ascertain whether they were still living there, and,
in case of their being alive at the place, to return to me
with the information. I had nearly terminated my arrangements concerning the new town, when the vessel came back,
bringing on board the procurador and one of the regidores
or aldermen of the town, who, having come to my presence,
begged me most earnestly, in the name of their fellow-citi-
zens, to go and help them, as they were in the utmost dis-

tress, owing to the following circumstances which they explained to me :—It would appear that the captain appointed by Francisco de las Casas, when he went away, and an alcalde whom he had likewise placed over the town, had taken possession of a vessel then in the harbour, and, out of one hundred and ten settlers, had persuaded fifty to follow them, leaving the remainder without weapons or iron tools of any sort, taking away besides almost everything they possessed, so that they were in great fear of either falling into the hands of the Indians, or being starved to death, for they had no means of providing for their wants. A vessel from Hispaniola, owned by the bachelor Francisco Moreno, had since arrived in those parts; but, although they applied to him for provisions and help, he had refused to give them any; as they would more amply inform me, if I only took the trouble of visiting them. Hearing the miserable plight to which those people were reduced, I again embarked with all the sick and wounded of my small army—though by that time some of them had died—it being my intention to send them from that place to the Islands and to New Spain, as I afterwards did. I took on board with me some of my own household servants, and gave orders besides that twenty horsemen and ten cross-bow-men should go by land, having heard that the road to the village was good and practicable, though they would have to pass some rivers on their way thither.

Having met with contrary winds at sea, it took me full nine days to arrive at the port of Honduras, where I anchored; and having gone into a boat with two Franciscan friars, who had always accompanied me, besides the Spaniards of my suite, made quickly for the shore, where the people of the town were already expecting me. As the boat came near to the shore, all those people jumped into the water, and took me out of the boat in their arms, showing every sign of happiness and joy at my coming. In this way we reached the

village, and entered a church, where, after thanking our
Lord and Saviour, they begged me to sit down and listen to
the narrative of the events that had occurred in that locality,
and the part they had taken in them, as they were under
the impression that I might have been misinformed respecting some of them individually, and be angry in consequence.
Thus, by hearing the truth, I might judge whether they had
acted wrong, and accept their excuses.

To this proposal I agreed, when a clergyman of theirs got
up and made the following oration, which I here transcribe
at full length :—" Sir : Your worship knows full well how
all of us who now are here were sent from New Spain, under
Christoval de Olid, your captain, to settle and populate in
this country, in the name of His Imperial Majesty ; and how
we were told to obey the commands of the said captain as if
they came directly from your worship. So we went along
with him to the island of Cuba, where we were to take certain provisions and horses that were still requisite for the
intended expedition. Having entered the harbour of La
Havana, in the said island, our captain communicated, by
letters,[1] with Diego Velasquez, the governor, and with his
Majesty's officers residing at the place, who procured him
some volunteers. After providing ourselves with everything
we wanted, through the agency of Alonso de Contreras,
your worship's servant, who supplied us, we quitted the
island, and continued our navigation. I will pass over in
silence some incidents of our voyage, as uninteresting and
tedious to narrate, and will go on to say how we arrived
on this coast, fourteen leagues lower than the port of Caballos, where, having landed, the said Christoval de Olid took
possession, in his Majesty's name and for your worship, of
all the country around, laying soon after the foundations of
a town, installing the alcaldes and aldermen already ap-

---

[1] Velasquez's residence at the time was Santiago de Cuba, formerly
the capital of the island.

pointed in New Spain, and doing other official acts respecting the possession and population of the said town, always
in your worship's name, and as your governor and lieutenant,
for such he was. Some days after this, he, the said Christoval de Olid, made common cause with various servants of
Diego Velasquez, who had accompanied the expedition from
Cuba, and went through certain formalities, by which it was
evident that he intended to shake off the obedience he owed
to your worship ; and, although most of us blamed him for
his conduct, we dared not remonstrate, because he threatened
us with the gallows, but, on the contrary, feigned to approve
of everything he did, especially when we saw that the very
relatives and servants of your worship, who formed part of
the expedition, had done the same; no doubt because they
were not prepared to offer any resistance. Having received
intelligence after this, through six messengers of Gil Gonzalez de Avila, another of your worship's captains, whom he
caused to be imprisoned, that the said captain, sent by your
worship, was coming down upon him in force, Christoval
de Olid went in person to wait for him at the ford of a
certain river, by which he had forcibly to pass. Having, however, waited some days in vain, he left one of his lieutenants
with some force, and returned to this town, where he began
to fit out two caravels, and to provide them with artillery
and ammunition, with the intention of attacking a village
higher up the coast, where some of the people of Gil Gonzalez had previously made a settlement. He was thus engaged, and preparing for this expedition, when Francisco
de las Casas unexpectedly entered the harbour with two
vessels. No sooner did Christoval de Olid ascertain who he
was, than he gave orders for the artillery of his caravels
to fire on him, which it did, albeit the said Francisco de
las Casas several times hoisted the flag of peace, and kept
crying at the top of his voice that he was your worship's
servant, and came there by your command. The artillery,

nevertheless, continued to play at the express order of Christoval de Olid, and ten or twelve shots were fired, one of which struck the side of one of the two vessels, and went through it. When the said Francisco de las Casas saw this act of open hostility against him and his men, he was fully persuaded that the rumours already current about Christoval de Olid's treason were quite certain, and that it would be a dangerous thing to temporise with such an enemy. He, therefore, prepared his guns, manned his boats, and, making his artillery play, took possession of those two vessels that were in the port, their crews having deserted them and fled on shore.

" When Christoval de Olid saw his vessels taken, and himself at the mercy of his enemy, he showed a disposition to come to terms, not indeed with any determination to end the affair amicably, but with a view to stop the said Francisco de las Casas in his doings until the forces he had sent against Gil Gonzalez de Avila should come back, not finding himself strong enough to cope with him. He, therefore, tried to deceive Las Casas, who, being of a confiding disposition, consented to everything he proposed.

" Matters were in this state, and the negociations between the two chiefs still far from coming to an end, when all of a sudden a great tempest arose at sea, and as there was no proper port at the place, and the coast was bad and full of shoals, the ship on board of which Francisco de las Casas was slipped her anchor, and was dashed against the shore, thirty-four of her crew being drowned. Las Casas and the rest of his men escaped in a state of almost complete nudity, and so ill-treated by the waves and lacerated by the rocks that they could scarcely keep their feet. In this plight they were brought to the presence of Christoval de Olid, who, having cast every one of them in irons, made them swear by the Holy Gospels that they would owe him obedience, look upon him as their captain and chief, and never afterwards go against his will.

" About this time news came how that field officer, whom
Christoval de Olid had stationed near the river which the
people of Gil Gonzalez had necessarily to pass, succeeded in
apprehending fifty-seven of them, commanded by an alcalde
mayor of that captain ; but he had, after some time, released
them all, allowing them to go one way, whilst he with his
men took another. Very much incensed at this, and hearing
that his orders had not been punctually executed, Christoval
de Olid started in the direction of Naco, where he had resided on a previous occasion, and took with him the said
Francisco de las Casas and some of his men, leaving the rest
of the prisoners under the care of a lieutenant and an alcalde,
whom he appointed for the purpose. Las Casas then begged
and entreated him several times, and in presence of all the
people, to let him go back to your worship and report on
what had taken place; for if he did not, he, Las Casas,
would try all means in his power to obtain his liberation ;
and therefore advised him to keep good watch on his person, and not to trust him. Notwithstanding his entreaties
and threats, Christoval de Olid never would let him go.

" Some days after, Christoval de Olid, having received
intelligence that Gil Gonzalez, followed by a few of his men,
had settled, and was residing at a neighbouring place on the
coast called Choloma,[1] sent against him some troops, and he
and all his people were made prisoners. In this manner did
Christoval de Olid secure and retain the persons of the two
captains sent by your worship to these parts, although both,
and each of them in particular, begged him several times to
let them go their own way. He, moreover, in a like manner,
made all those people of Gil Gonzalez swear that they would
from that day hold and consider him as their chief and captain.
As to Francisco de las Casas, many a time after the imprisonment of Gil Gonzalez did he address the said Christoval de
Olid in public, again entreating him to set him and his com-

---

[1] This is one of the villages mentioned at p. 96.

panions at liberty, for otherwise, he added, one day or other, and finding their opportunity at hand, they were sure to release themselves and put him to death. Christoval de Olid, however, never would listen to his threats, until the tyranny of that governor becoming intolerable even to his own people, the prisoners recovered their liberty in the following manner:—One night that the three captains—that is to say, Christoval de Olid and his two prisoners—were together in the same room, and several other people with them, Francisco de las Casas, who had been disputing rather violently with Olid on certain matters, rushed suddenly upon him, seized him by the beard, and, with a pen-knife that he held in his hand, for he had no other weapon with him, being at the time engaged in walking up and down the room and cutting his nails, gave him a cut across the throat, exclaiming, ' Down with the tyrant, and his tyranny! We have borne it too long.' This being done, he and Gil Gonzalez and others of your worship's servants, who were then in the room, ran upon the arms of the soldiers, formerly his body-guard, and a scuffle ensued, in which the said Christoval de Olid, the captain and ensign of his body-guard, his field-officer, and others, were wounded, or taken prisoners and disarmed, though not one of them was killed. Christoval de Olid, in the midst of the fray, managed to escape from the house, and hide himself somewhere ; but in less than two hours the above-mentioned captains succeeded in securing the persons of his principal adherents, and quieting the rest of the people, publicly proclaiming, by the voice of the crier, that whoever knew whereabout Olid lay concealed, should report it immediately under pain of death. He was soon after detected, and placed in irons, and on the morning of the following day, having gone through his trial in due form, he was sentenced to death, and, his sentence being signed by the two said captains, he was beheaded, to the great satisfaction of all the people, who thus recovered their liberty.

" Immediately after Olid's execution, it was proclaimed,
by public crier, that all those who wished to settle in this
country should inscribe their names, and that those
who wished to return to New Spain should also manifest their intentions. One hundred and ten settlers out of
the whole number declared their wish to remain and live
where they were ; all the rest said they preferred going back
to' your worship, either with Francisco de las Casas or with
Gil Gonzalez. Among those who chose to remain were
twenty Spaniards who owned horses, and to that number I
and all those who are here belong. Francisco de las Casas
provided us with everything we wanted, appointed a captain to command us, and bade us come to this coast and
colonise for your worship and in the name of his Imperial
Majesty. He also named alcaldes and aldermen, and a
scrivener, or notary, an attorney-general to the Municipality,
and an alguasil, and decided that the new town should be
called Trujillo, promising, and giving us his word as a
gentleman, that he would, as soon as possible, obtain for us
from your worship the requisite aid in men, arms, horses,
food, and other things necessary to keep the country at peace.
He, moreover, gave us two interpreters, one Indian and one
Christian, who understood very well the dialects of this
country. And thus we took leave of him, intending to
follow his instructions literally, whilst he, in order that your
Worship should be made sooner acquainted with his doings,
and assist us in our undertakings, despatched a ship with
the news.

" Having arrived at the port of Saint Andrew, also known
as Los Caballos, we found there a caravel that had recently
come from the Islands, and as, in that place, there did
not seem to us to be a proper spot to found a town, and
we knew of a better one, we freighted the said caravel to
take down all our heavy luggage, and our captain went on
board of her with about forty of his men and all our provi-

sions and heavy goods, whilst those who, like us, had horses, and the rest of the people, followed by land, with no other apparel but that which we had on, in order to travel more at ease, and lest we should meet with an accident on our journey. The captain, nevertheless, gave his full powers to one of the alcaldes, the same who now is here with us—for the other one went with him in the caravel—to command during his absence. In this manner we parted company, intending to join afterwards at this port; but when, after a troublesome and fatiguing march, during which we had many an encounter with the natives, and one above all more serious than the rest, in which two Spaniards and some of the Indians we had with us were killed, we were greatly surprised to find no vessel in the port.

"As I have had the honour to inform your worship, we arrived at the place appointed for our meeting in the most miserable condition, with our clothes all torn, and our horses fatigued and unshod, yet we were happy and contented, because we expected to find there the caravel with our captain and the rest of the men, our arms and luggage. But what was our disappointment and dismay when we saw that the caravel was not in port, and knew that all our necessaries, such as provisions, clothes, iron tools, and other valuables, were in the missing ship! We remained for some time stupefied and without knowing what resolution to take, until, having consulted together, we decided to wait at the spot for the succours which Francisco de las Casas had promised in your worship's name, and which we were sure would come sooner or later. And so we went on building the town, and took possession of the surrounding country in his Majesty's name, and had a legal act of the whole ceremony drawn before the notary of the municipality, as your worship may verify.

" Five or six days after, there appeared at sea, about two leagues from this place, a caravel; and having sent our

alguazil in a canoe to know whose she was, she proved to be
under the command of a certain Francisco Moreno, a re-
sident at Hispaniola, and a bachelor in law, who had
come hither by order of the judges there exercising the
royal authority, for the purpose of inquiring into certain
business between Christoval de Olid and Gil Gonzalez. It
further appeared that the caravel was well stocked with provisions, arms, and ammunition, the property of his Imperial
Majesty. We were delighted at hearing this good news,
and thanked our Lord most heartily for it, not doubting that
we were forthwith to be remedied in our extreme want.
Having therefore sent to the caravel the alcalde, the aldermen, and some of the principal citizens, that they might describe our miserable situation, and beg the said bachelor
Francisco Moreno to give us help, we were excessively
grieved to see that he not only flatly refused to receive our
deputation on board, but manned the sides of the ship,
though he consented at last that four of the party, without
arms, should go on board and deliver their message, which
we did in the best possible terms, informing him how we were
settled in this town by order of your worship and in his
Majesty's name, and how, in consequence of our captain
having gone away in the caravel with everything we possessed in the world, we had been left in a state of utter
destitution, having neither provisions, arms, iron tools,
nor clothes. That we firmly believed that God had brought
him to the spot for our remedy; and since, as we had been
informed, the cargo in the caravel belonged to his Majesty,
we begged and entreated him to provide us with the necessaries of life, by which he would do service to his Majesty
and to your worship, and at the same time not lose anything, for we bound ourselves to pay him the price of every
thing he gave us. To this he answered that he was not
come hither to provide for our wants, and would not give us
anything unless we paid him on the spot in gold or slaves.

" Two merchants who were in the caravel, and a certain
Gaspar Troche, from the island of Saint John, then tried to
interfere in our favour, asking the said Moreno to give us
what we wanted, and offering to stand security for the payment to the amount of five or six thousand castellanos, to be
delivered at such periods as he would fix. They further told
him that he well knew they had sufficient property to take
such an engagement, and that in doing so they believed they
did a service to his Majesty, besides being agreeable to your
worship, who, they had no doubt, would repay their advances
and be grateful for the service. Not even then, solicited as
he was by those people, would he consent to give or sell us
anything he had on board; but on the contrary, bade us go at
once, and literally put us out of his caravel, saying that he
wanted to make sail and go away. He however sent after
us one named Juan Ruano whom he had in his company,
and who had been the principal instigator of Christoval de
Olid's treason. This Ruano communicated secretly with the
alcalde, with the aldermen, and with some of us also, promising that if we would only follow his advice, he would not
only induce bachelor Moreno to give us everything we
wanted, but that on his return to Hispaniola, he, Ruano,
would obtain from the judges there residing that we should
not have to pay for anything, and that he would besides
have us provided from that island with men, arms, horses,
food, and all the necessaries of life. That if we did as he
told us, the same bachelor Moreno would soon return to us
with all those things, and sufficient powers also from the
judges to become our chief and captain. Having then asked
him what he expected us to do in return, Ruano answered
that we were before all things to depose from their respective charges the alcalde, the aldermen, the treasurer and
accounting master, besides the inspector and all the other officials who were there in representation of your worship's
authority. After this we were to apply to the said bachelor

Moreno to appoint him, Ruano, for our captain, saying that
we were determined to obey in future the orders of the
Audiencia, and not those of your worship.   We were to
make a petition to this effect, and sign it with all our names,
including an oath of allegiance to the said Juan Ruano, and
a promise that if any people or messengers came from your
worship, we were not only to disobey their orders, but even
to take up arms in our defence.

"Our answer to such propositions was that it was impossible
for us to accept, since we had taken a different oath.   That
we were here settled for his Majesty, and in your worship's
name, as his captain and governor, and could not do what
they asked from us.   To this answer of ours the said Juan
Ruano replied that he again begged us to consider whether
it was not better for us to accept his proposals than die
through starvation.   For certainly, he added, Moreno will
never give you a morsel of bread or a jug of water as long
as you persist in your refusal, having already announced his
determination to set sail and go away.

" Hearing this, we again met together, and compelled by
want, came to the resolution of granting everything that man
asked rather than expose ourselves to certain death through
starvation, or at the hands of the natives, for we had no
weapons wherewith to defend ourselves.   We therefore told
Ruano that we were ready to comply with his wishes, and
that he could at once return to the caravel and announce
our intention.   He did so, and soon after the said bachelor
Francisco Moreno came on shore, followed by many armed
people, and Juan Ruano had a petition drawn before the
notary of the place, signed by almost every one of us, and
strengthened by our oaths, in which we asked him, Ruano,
to be our captain and governor ; after which the alcalde, the
aldermen, the treasurer, the accounting master, and veedor
resigned their respective offices, and the name of the town
was changed—being called Ascension instead of Trujillo—

and certain official deeds were drawn whereby it appeared
that we were there settled under the authority of the judges
at Hispaniola, and not on your worship's account.

"The above deeds being passed and signed, the said bachelor
supplied us with everything we wanted, and ordered a foray
to be made into the districts surrounding our settlement,
when we brought in a certain number of prisoners, who,
being marked with a hot iron as slaves, he afterwards took
away with him. He even refused to pay the fifth that was
due to his Majesty, ordering that in future there should be
neither treasurer, nor accounting master, nor inspector to collect and receive the royal rights, but that the said Ruano—
whom he left over us as captain—should be the sole receiver,
without any sort of control or book-keeping. And this
being done, he sailed for Hispaniola, leaving, as I have
already related to your worship, the said Juan Ruano to
command over us, under certain requisitory clauses in case
any forces sent by your worship came to these parts, promising at the same time to return soon with such an army
that nobody would dare to resist the authority of the judges,
in whose name those measures were taken.

"No sooner, however, had Moreno departed, than persuaded
as we all were that the above acts and deeds were contrary to the service of his Majesty, we seized on the person
of the said Juan Ruano, and sent him a prisoner to the
islands, after which the alcalde and aldermen again filled
their respective offices as before, and we have since been,
and are still, subject to your worship's orders in his Majesty's
name, humbly asking your worship to pardon our mis-
demeanours in the time of Christoval de Olid's time, because
we were also compelled by force, and could not act otherwise."

The address being ended, I answered those people that
the offences in Christoval de Olid's time I fully forgave in
his Majesty's name, and as to more recent acts, they were

not guilty of any, since they had been compelled by hunger
and utter destitution ; but that they were in future to abstain from all similar revolutions and scandals, by which
they would no doubt incur your Majesty's displeasure, and
bring on themselves the condign punishment for all offences,
past as well as present.   And in order more fully to impress
them with my disposition to forgive, and forget even the
events in which they had been concerned, as well as with
my readiness to favour and assist them with all my might—
provided always that they would continue the faithful vassals
of your Majesty—I forthwith confirmed in their respective
offices, and in the royal name, the alcaldes and aldermen
who had been appointed by Francisco de las Casas, acting
as my lieutenant.   At all of which they were very much
rejoiced, without fear of being ever questioned as to past
offences.

Having, however, represented to me that Moreno would
shortly come back upon them with considerable forces, and
new provisions from the judges residing at Hispaniola, I
did not then move from the port, that I might be ready to
protect them in case of need ; but seeing that he did not
make his appearance, and having received certain information respecting the Indians in the immediate neighbourhood,
I gave all my attention to the affairs of the new settlement.
I learned through the Spaniards that at about six or seven
leagues from the town there were certain villages of Indians
with whom they had had skirmishes, whenever they had
gone that way in search of provisions.   Some of the natives,
however, were better disposed than others for peace ; for
although they had no interpreter to converse with them,
they had shown by signs their good will and friendship.   No
doubt that if these people were spoken to by a person who
knew their language, they might be easily reduced, although
they had on several occasions been ill-used, the Spaniards
taking from them certain women and boys, the same that

bachelor Moreno had marked with a hot iron as slaves, and taken away in his ship.

God knows how much grieved I was by such intelligence, knowing full well the great evils that might ensue from these proceedings. I, therefore, by the vessels I sent to Hispaniola, wrote to the judges of that island, complaining about the said bachelor Moreno, and enclosing a written testimonial of all the misdeeds executed by him in that town and its immediate neighbourhood, besides certain requisitory letters in which I enjoined them—as your Majesty's captain-general in these parts of New Spain—to send to me the said bachelor Francisco Moreno, a prisoner and in irons, together with all the natives of this province, whom he had taken as slaves in direct violation of the laws promulgated on that subject, as was fully proved by the papers and documents which I also sent. I do not know what the said judges will decide on my application: of their resolution, if they take any, I shall not fail to inform your Majesty.

Two days after my arrival at this port and town of Trujillo, I sent to those villages in the neighbourhood, which the settlers had mentioned to me, a Spaniard and three Indians from Culua, who knew their dialect well, and to whom I gave my full instructions as to what they were to say to the chiefs and natives of the said villages, namely, who I was, and how I had arrived among them; for, owing to the great traffic there was in those parts, many people had learned through merchants and traders my doings in Mexico. Among the first villages visited by these messengers of mine, there was one called Champagua,[1] and another Papayeca,[2] which are seven leagues distant from Trujillo, and two from each other. They were both considerable, as we have since ascertained, because the latter,

---

[1] This name is sometimes written Chapagua, the sign for the m being omitted.

[2] Sometimes Papayecua and Papayegua.

Papayeca, has eighteen small villages appertaining to it, whilst Champagua had ten. It pleased, however, our Lord and Saviour—who, as we know by daily experience, takes especial care of us—that the inhabitants of Papayeca should listen with great attention to my embassy, and send along with those messengers of mine certain numbers of their people, to learn the truth of what my interpreters had told them. They were very well received by me, and having presented them with some trifles, I again addressed them through the interpreter I had with me; for it was found that their dialect and that of Culua do not differ essentially, and are almost one and the same, with the exception of a few words, and some slight change in the pronunciation. I repeated to them what my messengers had already said, adding a few things that I considered necessary to inspire them with greater confidence, and begged them very earnestly to persuade their chiefs to come and see me, with which they took leave, and went away very contented. Five days after this a principal Indian, by name Montamal,[1] and who, as it was found out afterwards, was the chief of a village called Telica, in the district of Champagua, came to see me; whilst on behalf of Papayeca and its province there came another Indian, named Cecoatl,[2] who was also chief of Coabita,[3] a village in that neighbourhood. They both brought me some provisions, consisting of maize, fowls, and some fruit, saying that they came sent by their respective lords to know what I wanted, and what was the cause of my visiting their country. They did not come personally because they were afraid of being taken on board the ships and sent away, as the Christians who first landed on that shore had done with certain countrymen of theirs. I told them how grieved I was to hear of that outrage, which had been perpetrated without

[1] The name of this chief is also written Montuval.
[2] Elsewhere Cecoaël and Lecoalt.
[3] In the Vienna copy "Coabata."

my knowledge, promising them from that day that no injury
or harm should be done unto them, and that I even intended
to send for those who had been carried away, and restore
them to their homes. May it please God that the licenciates at
Hispaniola allow me to keep my engagement with those
Indians! though I very much fear that they will not send
back to me those slaves taken by Moreno, but, on the contrary, will find some expedient to palliate his crime, believing, as I do, that the said bachelor acted according to
instructions received from the Audiencia, and did nothing
except by express orders.

In answer to the question which those messengers put to
me respecting my object in coming to that country, I told
them that they ought to know how, about eight years before
that time, I had arrived in the province of Culua, and how
Muteczuma, then lord of the great city of Tenuxtitlan and
of all that country, being informed by me of the greatness
and power of your Majesty—to whom the universal world
is subjected—and of my having been sent to visit this
country to propagate the fame of your royal name, had received me very well and acknowledged at once what was
due to your Majesty ; that all the other lords in the country
had done the same. I then narrated to them that part of
my doings which I thought most fit for the present object,
and concluded by letting them know that my mission was to
visit all and every one of the provinces of that great continent, without omitting one, and to found, wherever I considered it beneficial, towns and cities of Christians, who were
to teach them the best mode of living for the preservation of
their persons and property, as well as for the salvation of
their souls. That this, and no other, was the cause of my
coming, through which they might be certain no harm would
result to them, but on the contrary much good, since all
those who obeyed your Majesty's royal commands would be
well treated and maintained in justice, whilst the rebels

should be severely punished.   Many other things I told them to the same purpose, which, in order not to annoy your Majesty with too much writing, I shall omit, especially as they are not of great importance.

I gave these messengers a few trifles, such as they generally hold in great esteem, though they have hardly any value among us, and they returned to their respective villages very happy and contented.   And because I begged them when they went away to send me people who might help in levelling the site of the town, which was placed on a great mountain, they soon after returned with a number of men, and a sufficient quantity of fresh provisions.   Yet with all this their chiefs came not to visit me.   This I took no notice of, making as if their coming were a matter quite indifferent to me, though I desired them to send messengers to all the neighbouring villages to announce what my intentions were, and what I had told them on a former occasion, and begged that they would provide me with work-people for the new town.   My request was complied with, and in a few days' time there came, from fifteen or sixteen villages or rather lordships in that vicinity, people enough to help us efficiently in our works, bringing with them a sufficient quantity of fresh provisions to last us until the vessels I had sent to Hispaniola should return.

About this time I despatched for home the three ships I had with me, besides another one which came afterwards and was bought by me, and I sent in them all the invalids and sick people of the expedition.   One of the vessels arrived at a port of New Spain, and in her was a letter of mine to the royal officers I had left in command during my absence, as well as to the municipalities of the different towns, informing them of my operations and doings, and telling them how I was under the necessity of delaying a little longer in those parts; I recommended them particularly some of the matters left to their care, and offered my advice in others.

To the master of this vessel I gave orders to return by way of Cozumel, an island on the way, and to pick up certain Spaniards whom one Valenzuela had abandoned in that place. These were reported to be more than sixty in number, and to have formed part of the vessel's crew which mutinied with Valenzuela and sacked the first settlement made on the coast by Christoval de Olid. The other vessel, which I bought last in the small bay adjoining our town, I sent to the island of Cuba and to the town of Trinidad for a cargo of salted meat, horses, and volunteers, with orders to return as quickly as they could. A third was sent to Jamaica for the same purpose. The large caravel or brigantine, which I myself built (at Nito) I dispatched to Hispaniola, and in her was a servant of mine, bearer of letters for your Majesty, and for those licentiates (of the Audiencia) residing in the island. But, as it was found out afterwards, not one of those vessels reached her destination, because the one bound for Cuba and Trinidad was obliged by contrary winds to touch at Guaniguanico, and her crew had to go by land to the Havana, a distance of about fifty leagues, for a cargo. When this last mentioned vessel, the first that returned, entered the port of Trujillo, I learned from her crew that the one sent to New Spain, after taking on board the people of Cozumel, had gone on shore near a cape on the coast of Cuba, called San Anton or Corrientes, everything on board of her being lost, and most of her crew drowned, including a cousin of mine, Juan de Avalos by name, who went in command of her, and the two Franciscan friars who had accompanied my expedition, and thirty-four more people, whose names they gave me in writing. The few saved from the shipwreck had wandered through the neighbouring mountains without knowing where to go, and had mostly died of starvation. Out of eighty-four living souls only fifteen remained, who had arrived at that port of Guaniguanico, where my other ship was then at anchor.

There happened to be close at hand a sort of farm belonging to a Spaniard domiciliated at the Havana, where the said vessel was at the time taking in her cargo of provisions; a circumstance which greatly contributed to the saving of those poor wretches, for they were immediately supplied with what they wanted.

God only knows the sorrow I experienced at hearing of such a disastrous shipwreck; for besides losing through it a number of friends, servants, and relations, besides a large stock of breastplates, muskets, crossbows, and other weapons, my despatches never reached your Majesty's hands, which was a thing of the greatest consequence to me, as I will show hereafter.

The vessel bound for Jamaica and the one I sent to Hispaniola arrived at Trinidad in the island of Cuba, where they met with the licenciate Alonzo de Zuazo, whom I had left as chief justice, and with one of the governors of New Spain during my absence, and they found likewise in the port a vessel which those licenciates residing at Hispaniola were on the point of despatching to New Spain, for the purpose of ascertaining whether the news reported of my death were true or not. However, as the people of the vessel fitted out by the oidors[1] knew that I was alive, they changed their course and arrived where I was; for having on board thirty-two horses, and some saddles fit for riding in the *gineta* or Moorish style, besides a certain quantity of provisions, they thought they might sell them better to me than anywhere else.

By this vessel I received a letter from the said Alonzo Zuazo, informing me that among the officers of your Majesty in New Spain there had been great dissensions and scandals, the said officers having given out that I was dead; in conse-

---

[1] *Oidores*, or auditors, were the judges composing the Audiencia or court of the island. Cortes calls them generally *licenciados*, because they were so graduated.

quence of which, two of them had proclaimed themselves
governors, making the people swear and acknowledge them
as such. They had, moreover, imprisoned the said licenciate
Alonzo Zuazo, and the two other crown officers, as well as
Rodrigo de Paz, whom I had left in charge of my house and
property. This they had completely confiscated, removing
besides the alcaldes and judges nominated by me, and
appointing others of their own party. Many other particulars the letter contained, which being too long to relate, I
omit in this writing of mine, referring entirely to Zuazo's
original, which accompanies this.

Your Majesty may easily conceive what my feelings were
on the receipt of such intelligence, especially when I heard
of the ingratitude of those people, and the manner in which
they rewarded my services to the crown; pillaging my house
and property, and committing other rash acts, unjustifiable
even had I been dead; for although they may give out
as an excuse that I owe to the royal coffers more than sixty
thousand castellanos of gold, they know as well as I do
that I am no real debtor for that sum, but on the contrary
the imperial treasury owes me one hundred and fifty thousand
that I have spent out of my own pocket—and I may venture
to add not altogether unprofitably—in your Majesty's service.

My first thought, on hearing this news, was to sail in that
very ship that brought me Zuazo's letter, and punish the
guilty parties accordingly; for now-a-days every man who is
abroad and holds an office fancies that unless he does act independently and on his own account he is no gentleman at
all.[1] A similar thing, I hear, has just happened to Pedro Arias
[Davila] with a captain of his whom he sent to Nicaragua,
and who has of late completely thrown off his allegiance, as
will hereafter inforn your Majesty more at full. But on the
other hand it was exceedingly painful to me to leave that

[1] *Que si no hacen befa, no portan penacho*, is the graphic expression
used by Cortes, borrowing a simile of the old tournaments.

country in the state it then was, for had I done so, I am certain that all the benefits hereafter to be derived from the settlement would have been irrevocably lost, whereas, on the contrary, I am persuaded that it will turn out in time to be in fertility and riches a second Culua; for I have trust-worthy reports of very extensive and rich provinces, and of powerful chiefs ruling over them, and of one in particular, called Hueitapalan,[1] and in another dialect Xucutaco,[2] about which I possessed information six years since, having all this time made inquiries about it, and ascertained that it lies eight or ten days' march from that town of Trujillo, or rather between fifty and sixty leagues. So wonderful are the reports about this particular province, that even allowing largely for exaggeration, it will exceed Mexico in riches, and equal it in the largeness of its towns and villages, the density of its population, and the policy of its inhabitants.

In this perplexity, and not knowing what resolution to take, I bethought me that no human action in this world can turn to good except it be guided by the hand of the divine and primary cause of all things created. I, therefore, ordered masses to be said, and processions of priests to be made, most humbly praying God that he would inspire me with the line of conduct most acceptable to Him; and these pious exercises being continued a few days longer, after mature reflection, I resolved to put aside any other conside-ration, and start at once for Mexico in order to put a stop to the evils that afflicted this country. Leaving, therefore, as my lieutenant in the town of Trujillo, a cousin of mine, named Hernando de Saavedra, (brother of that Juan de Avalos, who was drowned in coming to that place) and placing under his

[1] Thus written in all the copies, but I should suggest that Hueitapatlan should be read instead, this one appearing to me a more Indian termi-nation.

[2] The Vienna copy reads Axucutaco.

orders thirty-five horse and about fifty foot; giving him
my instructions as to the manner in which he was to govern;
having likewise taken leave of some of the Indian chiefs who
had by that time visited me, and seemed very well disposed
and peaceable, I went on board the said vessel, with all my
household servants; after having sent orders to the people of
Naco to follow along the shore the same route taken by
Francisco de las Casas, that is to say the south coast, and
come out at the place where Pedro de Alvarado was settled,[1]
that road being then quite known and secure, and the men
in sufficient numbers not to fear any attack from the natives.
I also sent certain instructions to the town called Navidad de
Nuestra Señora, and being already embarked and about to
set sail, with the last of my anchors slung, the wind
suddenly subsided, and my vessel could not clear the
harbour. On the morning of next day news came that
among the people I left settled in that town, there were
certain rumours of disapproval of my conduct, and which it
was to be feared might, after my departure, bring on some
scandal and dissension. Hearing which, and seeing that I
could not put to sea, I at once landed, and causing a legal
inquiry to be made, punished the malefactors, and every
thing was quiet again.

Two days was I detained for want of a fair wind to leave
the port, but on the third, a favourable breeze springing up,
I again embarked, and set sail. I had, however only proceeded two leagues on my voyage, when just as we were
doubling a very long point in which the harbour terminates,
the mainmast of my ship was split in two, and we were again
obliged to return to port to have it mended. This operation
lasted three days, at the end of which we again put to sea,
with favourable weather. We had sailed for two nights and
one day, and made fifty leagues or more, when we were

---

[1] That is to say, to Santiago de Guatemala, where Alvarado was supposed to be at the time.

suddenly assailed by contrary winds from the north; so strong
and powerful was the gale, that our foremast broke short
off, and I was the third time obliged, though with considerable trouble and difficulty, to return to port. Once
within, we thanked God for His mercy, for certainly we had
been on the point of shipwreck. We arrived, however, so
tempest-tost and worn out by the sea, that we had necessarily to take some rest, and therefore, whilst the damage
in the vessel was being repaired, I went on shore with all
the crew. But when I reflected that having put to sea thrice
with fine weather, I had been obliged as many times to return
to the port, I began to think that God was not willing that I
should leave that country in its present state. I was the
more persuaded of this, that I learned that some of the Indian
populations, whom I had left peaceably disposed, began about
that time to stir and show signs of discontent. I again commended everything to the hands of the Almighty, ordered
new processions, had masses said, and having reflected on the
matter, I came to this conclusion : that by sending on that
vessel, which I had destined for my passage to New Spain,
with full powers to my cousin Francisco de las Casas, and
letters for the corporations of the several towns, and for your
Majesty's officers, blaming them for their misdeeds ; by sending back also some of the principal Mexican Indians I had
with me, that they might certify to their countrymen of
my being alive, the object I had in view might be attained,
and the troubles in New Spain completely appeased. I took
my measures accordingly, and prepared everything, although
had I known at the time that the vessel I first sent was lost,
and with her my despatches about the South Sea, I might
perhaps have sent to Francisco de las Casas fuller instructions than I did.

The vessel, however, having sailed for New Spain, and my
health being very indifferent at the time, owing to what I
had suffered at sea, and from which I had not yet recovered,

I was unable to explore the neighbouring districts, as I would otherwise have wished. I, therefore, remained at Trujillo, first because I expected every day the return of the vessels I had sent to the islands in search of provisions ; and secondly, to attend to various matters concerning the building of the new town ; but I ordered my lieutenant to go with about thirty horse and as many foot and overrun the districts which I had intended to visit.

My men marched for five and thirty leagues through a beautiful valley, filled with many large and populous villages, abounding in all manner of native fruits, and well suited to grow any kind of cattle, as well as all the seeds and plants of our peninsula. They had no angry encounter with the natives ; on the contrary, having spoken to them through the interpreters, by means of those Indians in the neighbourhood who were already our friends, and accompanied the expedition, they succeeded in gaining their good will. In consequence of this no less than twenty chiefs of large villages came to visit me, and with great willingness offered themselves for subjects and vassals of your Majesty, promising to obey your royal commands, as they have since done, and are still doing, for to the very day of my departure I had always some of them with me, those who went away being immediately replaced by others who came, and brought provisions to the town, and did everything to be agreeable to us. May it please God to maintain them in their good will towards us, and guide them to those ends which are the constant object of your Majesty's wishes and mine—ends which I have no doubt they will reach, for things that begin well very rarely turn out amiss, and in the present case every good may be expected from the natives of those parts unless those who are called to command over them and administer justice treat them badly.

The two provinces of Papayeca and Champagua, which, as I have said before, were the first to offer us their friend-

ship, and to become your Majesty's vassals, were precisely
those in which some disturbance was apparent at the time
of my first embarkation. Seeing me come back, they were
somewhat afraid of me, and I had to send messengers of peace
to reassure them. Some of the natives of Champagua then
came to see me, not the chiefs; but as the majority of them
kept aloof, and removed from the villages their wives, their
sons, and their property, it was evident to me that they had
no confidence in us. Among those who came daily, there
were several who took service and worked in the town;
these I strongly requested to return to their homes, but they
never would, saying, "not to-day but to-morrow." But as that
to-morrow never came, I managed to lay hands on three of
their chiefs, named Chiwhuytl, Poto, and Mondoreto, and
having imprisoned them, I named them a certain period of
time during which they were to come down from their mountains and return to their villages as before, threatening, if
they did not, to have them chastised as rebels. They all
promised to do it, and I set them free in consequence, and I
must say that they have since fulfilled their word, for the
natives have returned, and they live in security and peace,
doing whatever service is required from them.

Those of Papayeca, however, never would consent to come
back, particularly their chiefs, who always kept the people
with them in the mountains, whilst their villages continued
deserted; although frequently requested and summoned by
me to return to their homes, they never would. Seeing which,
I sent to the very heart of their country a troop of horse,
and some infantry, besides a number of Indians, who had
been reduced and served under our orders. This force, commanded by one of my lieutenants, one night surprised one
of the two chiefs of the country, named Pizacura, and having
asked him why he was so disobedient and rebellious, refusing
to comply with my orders, he answered that he would have
returned to his village before, had it not been for a comrade

.iis named Mazatl, who had more influence than himself on the community, and would not consent to it, but that if they let him go, he would betray Mazatl's movements, so that he might soon be taken prisoner, and if he were once in our hands, and hanged, he had no doubt all the people of his district would peaceably return to their villages, for if he had no opposition on Mazatl's part, he would easily induce all the natives of that province to do what we wanted. My lieutenant then set Pizacura at liberty, who did what he promised, and was the cause of greater misfortunes to his people than we might then have imagined; for certain friendly Indians from among the natives of that country tracked the said Mazatl to the spot where he had taken refuge, and guided there some of my Spaniards, who secured his person. Having notified to him what his comrade Pizacura said about him, he was enjoined to make his people come down from the mountains, and return to their villages within a short period of time, which was fixed; but so obstinate and rebellious was he that he could never be persuaded to give his consent. He was accordingly tried in due form, and sentenced to death, which was publicly executed on his person. It proved a great admonition for the rest of the natives, for immediately after most of them returned to their homes, and there is now in the province no village that is not perfectly secure, the natives living in peace with their families and property, except, however, those of Papayeca, which never could be entirely reduced, as I said before.

After the release of Pizacura, legal proceedings were instituted against the inhabitants of that province, and war was carried on in their territory, about one hundred of them being taken prisoners and made slaves. Pizacura himself was of their number. I had him tried, but did not sentence him to death, although he deserved it, and brought him with me to this city, together with two other chiefs of vil-

¹ That is of Papayeca.

lages not entirely reduced, that they might see with their
own eyes how things were managed in this New Spain, how
we treated the natives, and how they served us, and might
report to their countrymen on their return. Pizacura died
of illness; the other two chiefs are doing well, and I intend
sending them back on the first opportunity that occurs.

With the imprisonment, however, of this Pizacura, and of
another youth, who seemed to be his natural heir, with the
punishment inflicted by those hundred and odd Indians, who
were made slaves, the province was completely pacified, and
when I left that country all the villages paid tribute, and
the inhabitants were divided between the Spaniards, serving
them, as it appeared, with perfect good will.

About this time there came to the town of Trujillo a captain with about twenty men of those I had left at Naco
under Gonzalo de Sandoval, or belonging to the company of
Francisco Hernandez, whom Pedro Arias Davila, governor
for your Majesty in those parts, had sent towards the province of Nicaragua.   From them I learned how a captain of
the said Francisco Hernandez had arrived at Naco with about
forty men, between horse and foot, with a view to reach the
port in the bay of Saint Andrew, where he expected to find
that bachelor Moreno, who, as I have already informed your
Majesty in another part of this letter, had been sent thither
by the judges of Hispaniola. The said bachelor, as it
appears, had written a letter to Francisco Hernandez, in-
viting him to revolt against his own superior and governor,
just as he had incited the people left by Gil Gonzalez and
Francisco de las Casas to revolt against me; and in consequence whereof that captain came there to see him on behalf of Francisco Hernandez, and concert the best manner
of shaking off the allegiance due to his governor, and give
it instead to those judges in Hispaniola, as it appeared
from certain letters he had with him.

I sent those people back to their settlement, giving them

a letter for Francisco Hernandez and his men, and particularly for some of the captains in his company whom I knew, telling them how reproachable and bad their conduct had been in allowing themselves to be cheated by that bachelor, assuring them that your Majesty would be very angry at what they had done, and many other things to that purpose which I thought might draw them and their captains from the wrong path in which they were engaged. One of the causes they alleged for their justification was their being at such a distance from the residence of the said Pedro Arias Davila, that they could not be provided with the commonest things, except with great difficulty and cost ; and that they were always in want of commodities and provisions from Spain, which could be more easily obtained through the settlements I had made on that coast ; adding that the said bachelor had written to them to say that all the country now acknowledged the authority of the Audiencia, and that he would soon return with plenty of men and provisions to confirm the said obedience. I told them that I would give orders to those settlements to furnish them with everything they might want, and to treat them amicably in their trade transactions, since they, and all of us, were equally your Majesty's vassals, and actually employed in the royal service ; but that all these offers of mine were only to be understood in case of their continuing in the obedience of their governor (Pedro Arias Davila), and not otherwise. And in order to show them that I was in earnest, and because they told me that what they most wanted was shoes for their horses and iron tools to work in the mines, I gave them two mules of mine loaded with such things to take back with them, and when they arrived at the settlement of Hernando de Sandoval,[1] that captain gave them two more mules of mine also loaded with iron work and tools.

After the departure of those Spaniards, there came to me,

[1] Elsewhere called Gonzalo, see above, p. 125.

from the province of Huilacho,[1] which is about sixty-five
leagues from the town of Trujillo, certain Indians who had on
a previous occasion sent me messengers offering themselves as
subjects and vassals of your Majesty. These people complained that a number of Spaniards, about twenty horse and
forty foot, followed by many Indians from other provinces,
who were their friends, had come suddenly to their villages'
and were daily inflicting on them every kind of outrage,
taking away from them their wives and children and robbing
their property. They begged me to remedy the evils they
were suffering, reminding me that, when they offered themselves as the vassals of your Majesty, I had promised them
every help and protection against those who wronged them.
Some time after, Hernando de Sandoval, my cousin, whom
I had left as my lieutenant in that part of the country, and
who was at that time pacifying the province of Papayeca, sent
to me two Spaniards belonging to that very party about whom
the Indians of Huilacho had complained. They had come'
they said, by orders of their captain to look out for the town
of Trujillo,[2] having been told by the natives that it was close
by, and that they would come without any fear, all the
country round it being at peace with us. From these
people I learned that the marauding party, commanded by
one Gabriel de Rojas, belonged to the division of the above
mentioned Francisco Hernandez, and that they had come,
in search of that port where I then was. Having thus
ascertained who the guilty parties were, I sent those two
Spaniards along with the natives of Huilacho who had made
the complaint, and one of my alguazils, to Gabriel de Rojas,

[1] Written also Huilancho and Huilcacho, evidently the same.

[2] Not far from Trujillo is the valley of Olancho, through which flows
a river called Guayape, famous for the quantity of gold diggings on its
banks; even now the best gold is procured from those parts. In some
of the maps I have consulted, and especially in that appended to Morelet's
Travels, a place called *Orlancho* is given, which might well be the one
here intended.

enjoining him forthwith to quit the province, and restore to the natives the property taken from them, as well as the women and children he had made captives of. I moreover wrote him a letter, saying that if he wanted anything, he had only to let me know, and I would immediately supply him and his men with it, provided always I had it at hand.

No sooner did Gabriel de Rojas read the summons I sent him through my alguazil, than in obedience to my orders, he quitted that province, and went elsewhere; at which the natives were much satisfied, though some time after they again came to me complaining that after the departure of my alguazil they had been visited by the same, or another, marauding party, who had again taken some of their people into captivity. This time I wrote to the above mentioned captain, Francisco Hernandez, offering to supply him and his men with anything they might want and I could procure, on condition, however, that he would maintain himself in obedience to his governor, Pedro Arias, and not molest those Indians who were living peaceably under my rule, and sure as I was by making him such commendations, to promote the interests of your majesty. How far the said captain has complied with my request since I left that coast, I am unable to say, but I learned from the alguazil I sent to Gabriel de Rojas, and from those who accompanied him, that one day the said Gabriel de Rojas received a letter from Francisco Hernandez, bidding him return in all haste with his men, as among those remaining with him much dissension had arisen, two of his captains, named Soto and Andres Garabito, having refused to obey him on the plea that he himself was about to shake off the allegiance due to Pedro Arias. Matters, however, remained in such a state that a split was inevitable, from which great evils might be apprehended for the Spaniards, as well as for the natives of that country. I leave it for your majesty to consider how much harm these riots and discord may do

to the royal interests, and how necessary it is to punish
with severity those who promote and are the cause of them.

Such being my firm belief, and knowing what service I
might render your majesty, if I succeeded in putting down
so great an evil, I decided to go in person to Nicaragua. I
was, therefore, preparing everything for my intended expedition, and opening a road through certain mountains I had
to traverse, when the vessel sent by me to New Spain
entered the port of Trujillo. There was on board of her a
cousin of mine, named fray Diego de Altamirano, a friar of
the order of Saint Francis; from what he himself told me,
and from the letters he brought, I learned the many disturbances, scandals, and dissensions which had arisen, and
were still existing at Mexico, between the royal officers,
whom I had left to govern during my absence; and how
necessary it was that I should immediately repair thither, in
order to stop, if possible, the progress of the evil. I was,
in consequence, obliged to give up all idea of going to
Nicaragua, and returning, as I had intended, the way of the
South Sea, in doing which I firmly believe that much service to God first, and afterwards to your majesty, might have
been done, owing to the many extensive and rich provinces
that lie betwixt, and which, though reduced and at peace for
the most part, might have been confirmed in their vassalage
by my thus going through them, especially those of Otlatan
and Guatemala, where Pedro de Alvarado always resided,
and which, having rebelled in consequence of various offences
done to them by the Spaniards, have never since become
peaceable, but on the contrary have done, and are still doing,
much harm to the Spaniards settled in their neighbourhood,
and to their Indian friends. For your Majesty must know
that the country there is very broken, and the population
very dense, and the people so warlike and brave, and at the
same time so trained in all kinds of warfare, offensive as
well as defensive, that they have invented pits and other

engines to kill the horses; and although the said Pedro de
Alvarado has never ceased making war upon them with upwards of 200 horse and 500 foot, all Spaniards, besides
5,000, and at other times even 10,000 Indians, he has hitherto
been unable to reduce them under your Majesty's rule, but,
on the contrary, they become every day stronger through
the people who join them. I believe, however, that if, God
permitting, I were to go among them, I could, by mild treatment or otherwise, bring them to a knowledge of what
they owe to your Majesty; for some provinces of this New
Spain, which rose in arms during my absence, owing to bad
treatment received from the Spaniards, and against which
marched no less than one hundred and twenty horse, and
300 foot, with a considerable train of artillery, beside many
thousand Indian auxiliaries, all under the command of the
veedor, who then governed in Mexico, not only persisted in
their rebellion, but defeated our army several times; whereas
with a simple message, that I sent them on my return, the
principal inhabitants of that province, Uttatlan[1] by name,
came and explained to me the cause of their rising; which
seemed to me just enough, namely, that the Spaniard to
whom they had been given in charge had burnt alive eight
of their principal chiefs, five of them having died on the
spot, and the remaining three a few days after; and although
they had demanded reparation and justice, it had not been
granted to them. I consoled them and treated them in such
a manner that they went away satisfied and contented, being
at the moment I write as quiet and peaceful as they were
before my departure for Honduras. I also have reasons to
believe that other Indian villages in the province of Coazacoalco, which are in the same rebellious mood, on hearing
of my arrival, and without my sending messengers to them,
will become quiet and peaceable.

I have already, in another part of my narrative, most

[1] Written also Coatlan.

Catholic Majesty, alluded to certain small islands, called Los Guenejos, opposite the port of Honduras, some of which are entirely deserted, owing to the several landings which the people of the islands have effected in them for the purpose of making slaves of the inhabitants. Some of them, however, still preserve a population, although scanty; and as I was informed that both at Cuba and at Jamaica, they had just fitted out an expedition to complete the devastation of the land and carry away as slaves the few inhabitants that remained, I sent a caravel with orders to look out for the Cubans, and request them in your Majesty's name not to land in those islands and harm the inhabitants, because I intended to reduce them by mild treatment to your Majesty's service, having heard through some who had come on the mainland that they were peaceably disposed. The said caravel met in one of the islands, called Huititla, another caravel belonging to the people of Cuba, and the commander of which was one Rodrigo de Merlo. The captain of mine found means to bring him to my presence with all the people he had taken captive. These I immediately released and sent back to their homes, and did not proceed criminally against the master of the vessel, because he showed me the written permission he had from the governor of Cuba, who had been properly authorised by the judges residing at Hispaniola. I, therefore, dismissed him and his crew, without doing them any more harm than setting at liberty the slaves they had taken; but the captain and most of those who came in his company, liking the country much, did not return to Cuba, and settled in that province, becoming citizens of one or other of the towns I had founded on that coast.

The chiefs of those islands, seeing the good service I had done them, and knowing also by those of their countrymen who were on the mainland how well they were treated, came to thank me for the benefits received, and offered themselves as subjects and vassals of your Highness, asking me to point out to them those things in which they could be useful to me and my people. I ordered them, in your Highness's name, to cultivate their fields as well as they could, for in reality they cannot be of any other use to us. And so they went away, taking back with them for each of those islands a written order of mine, notifying to the Spaniards who might arrive there, that they were to be considered as your Highness's vassals, and in no manner to be molested. They asked me besides for a Spaniard to reside with them in each of the islands, and although I could not then see to the matter, owing to the shortness of my departure, I left it for Hernando de Saavedra, my lieutenant, to provide, together with other things.

All matters being arranged, I went on board the ship that brought me the news of this city, and in her, and in two more vessels, which I had then in the port, embarked some of the people who had accompanied me in that expedition. We were only twenty in number, with our horses, because the greater part of my people preferred to settle in those towns, and the rest were already waiting for me on the road, believing that I would take the land route. I sent them a message to proceed on their march, informing them of my intended departure by sea and the cause of it. They have not yet arrived, but I have certain news of their coming.

All things concerning the administration of the new towns being thus provided for (though not so firmly as I could have wished, and as would have suited the royal service, which caused me considerable uneasiness and regret), I set sail with the three ships on the 25th day of April. At first my navigation was attended with such luck that four days after my departure I found myself at 150 leagues from the port of Chalchicuela.[1] There I was assailed by a very strong gale, which did not let me proceed on my voyage. Thinking that

[1] This was the Indian name for the spot where the town of Vera Cruz was founded.

the wind would subside, I kept at sea a day and a night,
but the weather became so rough that I was compelled to
make for the island of Cuba, anchoring six days after in
the port of the Havana, where I landed, and was very well
received by the inhabitants, some of whom were my friends
since the time I resided among them. They all rejoiced at
my coming, and I was pleased to see them again. As the
vessels had suffered much, and were considerably knocked
about, it was deemed necessary to have them overhauled,
which operation kept me ten days in that place ; I even was
obliged to buy another vessel which was in the port,
being careened, and left mine there because she leaked considerably.

The day after my arrival at La Havana, a vessel entered
the port coming from New Spain ; on the second day there
came another, and a third the day after. I learned from
them all that the country was at peace, and that security
and tranquillity had returned since the death of the factor
and veedor, though they told me there had been some
slight riots, which had been put down, and their promoters
punished. I was delighted to hear the news, especially as
I was afraid that my forced return to Trujillo and consequent
delay at that town might have aggravated the evils and dissensions of which Mexico was long the theatre.

Having written,[1] though briefly, to your Majesty, I sailed
from the Havana on the 16th of May, taking with me about
thirty individuals, who had come secretly from this place,
and in eight days reached the port of Chalchicuela. I could
not go in, owing to a sudden change of the weather, but remained outside about two leagues off. That very day, when
night came on, having manned the boat of my ship, as well
as a brigantine which we had found abandoned at sea, I made
for the shore, landed without difficulty, and proceeded on foot
to the town of Medellin, distant four leagues from the point

---

[1] This, like many other of Cortes' letters, must have been lost.

of my landing; and without being seen or heard by any living creature in the place, went straight to thank Almighty
God for his favours. The people of the town, however, soon
heard of my coming, and were greatly rejoiced at seeing me,
as I was glad to see them. That very night I despatched
messengers to this city, as well as to all other cities and
towns in the land, informing them of my arrival, and making
certain provisions which I had considered necessary to promote your Sacred Majesty's interests and the good of the
land; and in order to take some rest and recover from
the fatigues of my long journey, stayed there eleven days,
during which time I was visited by many chiefs and
other principal persons, natives of these parts, who all seemed
rejoiced at my coming- I then started for this city, and was
on the road fifteen days, receiving all the time the visits and
congratulations of the natives, some of whom came from a distance of upwards of eighty leagues, having previously placed
their couriers on the road to be informed of my arrival, which
they expected. And so they flocked to me from all parts of
the country, far and wide, and they shed tears with me, and
said many affectionate and trying words, telling me what they
had suffered during my absence, and how badly they had been
treated ; and this they related with such emphasis and feeling
that it broke the hearts of all those who listened to their
narrative. And although, of all the complaints which these
Indians made to me of the injustice done to them, it would
be rather difficult to give your Majesty a full account, so
great are they in number and so aggravating in their circumstances, I might still point out a few well worthy of
your Majesty's notice, but I reserve them for a better occasion, to be related by word of mouth.

On my arrival at this city, both Spaniards and natives congregated from all parts of the land, and received me with as
much joy, and as many signs of happiness, as if I had been
their own father. The royal treasurer and the master-

accountant came out to meet me at the head of a considerable
troop of horsemen, and in good order, showing the same signs
of goodwill and contentment which the others had shown. I
went, preceded by them, to the church and monastery of St.
Francis, to return thanks to the Lord for having brought me,
after so many fatigues and dangers, safe among my own
people, and for having permitted that I should find this city,
once so disturbed by civil discord, now enjoying every peace
and security. I stayed six days at the convent and with the
friars, until I had confessed all my sins, after which I went to
my residence in the city.

Two days before my departure from the monastery, a messenger came from Medellin, announcing the arrival at the
port of that town of certain vessels ; and it was rumoured
that in one of them there came, by your Majesty's command,
a judge of inquiry. My informers added that they could
not tell me what the orders and instructions of the said
magistrate could be. I immediately thought that your
Catholic Majesty, knowing full well the disturbances, riots,
and disasters caused in this country by the very officers whom
I left to command in my name, and not being informed of
my return, had naturally sent the said magistrate to inquire
into the cause of such evils. God knows how much pleased
I was to think that such might be the cause of his coming
here, for it would have been exceedingly painful for me to
be a judge in such matters ; because, injured and illtreated
as I had been, and my property destroyed by these tyrants,
it seemed to me that any sentence of mine, however mild
and just, might be reckoned by the evil-inclined as partial
and dictated by passion, a thing of all others which I most
detest ; though, from what I have shown in all the acts of
my life, it seems to me that I could never have been so
severe as their criminal deeds required. I, therefore, despatched in all haste a messenger to that port of Medellin, to
know whether my surmise was true, ordering the lieutenant

and alcaldes of the place to receive and honour the said magistrate and his retainers, whatever his commission might be ;
and, since he came in your Majesty's name, to have him properly lodged and entertained at a house which I had in
the place, giving him and his people anything they might
want. This, however, as I afterwards learned, he would not
accept.

On the day after the departure of my messenger, which
happened to be the festival of Saint John, as I was wit-
nessing bull-fights, joustings with reeds, and other games
suited to the occasion, another messenger arrived from
Medellin, bringing me a letter from the said magistrate, and
another one from your sacred Majesty, by which I understood
the object of his coming, and how your catholic Majesty had
sent him to make inquiries into my acts during the time that
I have been governing this country. Great was my satisfaction at hearing that your Majesty so deigned to look into
my merits or deserts, and I also felt very grateful at the
benevolent terms in which your Highness announced your
royal intention and readiness to remunerate my small services. For both these favours I kiss one hundred thousand
times your catholic Majesty's royal feet, and may God, our
Lord, permit that I repay with my blood some portion of
the mercies so conferred upon me, and that your Majesty
may be persuaded of my sincerity in expressing such a
wish, for this alone would be sufficient reward for all my
services.

In the letter which the magistrate himself, whose name
was Luis Ponce, wrote to me, I was informed that he was
on the point of leaving for this city, and as there are two
principal roads leading to it, and he did not state which
of them he intended to follow, I sent to each of them servants of my household to wait upon him, and show him the
way. The said Luis Ponce, however, travelled in such
haste, that although my orders were executed with all pos-

sible dispatch, my people met him twenty leagues from this
city, and, although he received my messengers, as I am told,
with due courtesy, and was glad to see them, he would not
accept their services. At this I was sorry, because, owing
to his quick travelling, he well needed the assistance that
was offered to him, as I have afterwards been informed ; but,
on the other hand, I was glad, because the refusal seemed
to come from an honest and upright magistrate, about to
enter upon office and power, and who, coming to en-
quire into the acts of my administration, was unwilling, by
accepting my offers of service, to bring suspicion on himself.
He arrived one evening two leagues from this city, and passed
the night there, and after that I had prepared everything for
his reception the next morning, sent me word not to come
out to him, as he intended to dine where he had slept, but
to send him a chaplain to say a mass to him, which I did.
Suspecting that he did all this to avoid any public reception, I was on my guard, but he came so early in the morning, that, although I was quick enough in the saddle, with
my people, I met him in the centre of the city, whence we
rode together to the monastery of Saint Francis, and heard
our mass. This being done, I said to him that if he was
pleased to present there the royal instructions, of which he
was the bearer, he could do so, as all the members of the municipal corporation, as well as the treasurer, master-accountant,
and other of your Majesty's officers, were there with
me ; but he would not, saying that on the next day he
would exhibit them in due form. And so he did, for on the
morning after, when we were all congregated together in the
cathedral—the dean and chapter being present also—he,
the said Luis Ponce, exhibited the royal instructions, which I
and all those who assisted at the ceremony, held in our hands,
took to our lips, and placed on our heads, as is customary
in such cases, promising to obey and execute the prescrip-
tions therein contained, as coming from our legitimate

master and natural lord. All the regidors then put down their wands, and resigned their offices, all the other ceremonies being complied with, as your Majesty will see by the official acts drawn on the occasion by the municipal notary. This being done, the object of Luis Ponce's commission was publicly announced through the city, and read in the market square by the public crier, purporting that he was sent by your sacred Majesty to inquire into the acts of my administration.

I was seventeen days at Mexico without being asked a single question respecting my conduct as governor, during which time the said Luis Ponce, the magistrate and judge of inquiry, was taken with illness, he, and almost every one of those who came in that fleet; and the disease increasing, it was God's pleasure that he should die of it, together with upwards of thirty individuals, who had accompanied him from Spain. In that number were two Dominican friars who also came with him, and, moreover, at the date of my writing, there are still many people labouring under the same distemper, and in great danger of death; for the disease they brought with them in that fleet has proved almost equal to pestilence, having since attacked some inhabitants of this city, two of whom died with the same symptoms, whilst there are still many who have not yet recovered entirely.

After Luis Ponce's death, his burial and funeral being performed with the solemnity and honours due to a person of his importance, and who had come on your Majesty's errand, I was earnestly requested by the municipal corporation of this city, as well as by all the deputies of towns, who happened to be present, again to take into my hands the government of this country, in the same manner and with the same authority that I had held it on a former occasion. This they begged me to do in your Majesty's name, expounding various reasons why I ought to do it, and showing the inconveniences and evils that might result from my non-

acceptance, as your sacred Majesty will see by the copy of
their petition and other papers which accompany this; I
answered them in the negative, as will also appear from the
said copies, excusing myself for various motives; but they
insisted and renewed their petitions more strongly than ever,
showing the great evils that might ensue, if I did not grant
their request. I still held good, and have since firmly maintained the same purpose, though I imagine that there may
be reasons why I ought to accede to their demands. But,
wishing above all things that your Majesty should be convinced of my purity and fidelity towards the royal service,
this being the chief aim of all my actions, and knowing that
without your Majesty's esteem, all the good things of this
world are nothing to me, and that I would rather not live in
it,—I have always put aside any consideration that might
tempt my acceptance; and not only have I done this, but
have maintained with all my force in his office a certain
licentiate, called Marcos de Aguilar, whom the said Luis
Ponce brought with him from Spain as his alcalde mayor
(chief justice), and I have also requested and entreated him
to prosecute the inquiry into my acts to the end. This the
said licentiate has refused to do, alleging that he has not
sufficient powers for it; at which I am exceedingly sorry, for
there is nothing in this world I desire so much—and that
not without some reason—as to have your Majesty properly
informed of my virtues and sins, if I have committed any,
sure as I am that when your Majesty has taken full cogni-
zance of my acts, I cannot fail to be amply remunerated,
not indeed on account of my past services, small as they are,
but because your Majesty is bound to be munificent towards
one who, like me, has served you so well and with so much
fidelity.

I, therefore, humbly beseech your Majesty, with all the
earnestness of which I am capable, that this matter of the
inquiry to be instituted into my acts, should not remain in

suspense, and, as it were, under the veil of simulation, but, on the contrary, that all the good or bad part of my actions should be proclaimed and made public; because this being for me a point of honour to obtain which I have gone through so many trials, and exposed my person to so many dangers, God forbid that the foul tongues of envious and wicked people, should make me lose that which I most prize in the world. I, therefore, again entreat your Majesty not to consent that such a thing should take place; I ask for no other mercy in payment of my services, nor do I care to live without.

In my opinion, most catholic Majesty, since the time I entered into these transactions, I always have had many powerful rivals and enemies; yet, however strong their iniquity and malice, they have never been sufficiently strong to darken the notoriety of my services, and my constant fidelity. Seeing, however, that they could not effectually injure my reputation, those enemies of mine have sought two ways, by which, as it would appear, they have thrown a sort of mist before the eyes of your Majesty, and caused your Majesty to deviate from the catholic and holy purpose— always acknowledged by your Majesty—of remunerating my services. One of these ways is to accuse me of the crime of *lèse-majesté*, pretending that I do not obey your Majesty's royal commands, and hold not this newly conquered land in the royal name, but under my tyrannical sway, giving as a proof of their calumnies various false and diabolical reasons, entirely the inventions of their depraved minds. Yet were the said wicked people to look truly into my acts, and to be made impartial judges of my conduct, they could not do less than proclaim the very reverse of what their foul tongues have spread against me; for until this present day there has never been, nor shall be in future, any letter or command of your Majesty that has not been punctually obeyed and faithfully executed to the letter.

At this very moment the iniquity and malice of those who have thus calumniated me have become more manifest than ever ; because had things been as they report, I should certainly not have gone six hundred leagues from this city, through uninhabited districts and over dangerous roads, leaving the government of the country in the hands of those among your Majesty's officers whom I considered most zealous in the royal service—though their deeds did not certainly correspond to the idea and estimation I had of them.

The other way which these people have found of attacking my reputation is to say that the greater part of the natives of this country are my slaves, and that I treat them as such, and profit by their service and their work, by means of which I have amassed a large sum of money, in gold and silver, which I hoard up; that I have spent without necessity more than sixty thousand ounces of gold out of your Majesty's revenue, and have not remitted to Spain as much gold as was due to the royal treasury, keeping and retaining it with me under specious pretences and for purposes which I cannot accomplish. I really believe that such rumours about me being current, the said wicked individuals have not failed to give them a certain specious colouring, though it cannot be such as to give them the appearance of truth, and I trust that the slightest approach of the touchstone will be sufficient to discover the falsity of the metal.

As to their saying that I possess a large portion of the land, I own that this is true, and I have likewise had for my share a good sum and quantity of gold ; but I maintain that all I have received has been insufficient to relieve me from misery and poverty, being at the moment I write in debt for upwards of five hundred ounces of gold, without possessing one single dollar towards it ; because, if the yieldings have been considerable, the expenses have been greater, having consumed very large sums, not indeed in buying lands, or founding entails, or acquiring any sort of property for myself

and heirs, but in extending and enlarging your Highness's
patrimonial rights in these parts through the conquest and
acquisition of so many kingdoms and empires, achieved at my
own peril and risk, and with infinite trouble and danger of
my person.   This part, however, of my services their foul
and viperous tongues shall never touch or impair; for only
by looking at my account-books it will be found that upwards of 300,000 ounces of gold have been spent out of my
own fortune in such conquests and acquisitions.   It is true
that when that resource was exhausted, and I had no more
money of my own to spend, I availed myself of the sixty
thousand gold ounces belonging to your Majesty, not indeed
for my own personal use, for they never passed through my
hands, but to be paid on my warrants for the cost and expenses of these latter conquests.   Whether the said monies
have been rightly spent or not, it is not for me to say, the
facts being patent and known to every one.

As to what the said calumniators say about my not having
sent to your Majesty the rents and produce of this country,
I scarcely need show how false the accusation is, for I maintain—and it is a fact—that during the few years that have
elapsed since I first set my foot in this country, more
treasure has been remitted to Spain from it than from all the
islands and Tierra Firme put together, though discovered
and peopled more than thirty years ago at great cost and
expense to the Catholic kings, your predecessors.   Your
Majesty, however, has had no disbursements to make with
regard to this my conquest ; for not only have I sent to Spain
whatever sums were due to the royal treasury, but I have on
many occasions presented your Majesty with what was
really my own, and so have most of the people who serve
under my orders.   So when I first wrote to your Majesty
giving the news of my landing, and sent along with the
letter Alonso Hernandez Portocarrero, and Francisco de
Montejo, not only did I offer to your Majesty the fifth of the

spoil made on that occasion, but I delivered also what rightly belonged to me and my companions, considering it was but just that your Majesty should have the first-fruits of this conquest. When this city of Mexico was taken the first time, the Emperor Muteczuma being still alive, your Majesty received thirty thousand castellanos of gold, as your fifth of what was then obtained and made into ingots; and although the jewels and other valuable things were to be divided also, so that every one of us should have his share in the spoil, we were all of us, my men as well as myself, of opinion that there ought to be no division whatever, and that the whole of such spoils, amounting in value to five hundred castellanos of gold, should be forthwith sent to your Majesty. True it is that everything, money and jewels, was lost when the people of this city rose in arms against us, and expelled us from it, owing to Narvaez's landing, but that mishap, if deserved through my sins, was certainly not owing to any negligence on my part. When, however, this city was taken for the second time, and its territory completely reduced under your Majesty's sway, the same course was followed. Of the gold that was smelted one fifth was put aside for the imperial treasury, and besides I persuaded my men to give up their share in the jewels and other valuable objects, amounting to a sum no less considerable than the one set out on the previous occasion. All these things, gold as well as jewels, in the shortest possible space of time, were by me entrusted to the care of Julian Alderete, then your Majesty's treasurer in these parts, as well as thirty-three thousand ounces of gold in ingots; but the whole of this treasure was taken by the French at sea. It was neither my fault, but the fault of those who did not fit out in time a sufficient naval force to send to the Azores for the protection of so important a remittance.

About the time of my starting on my latter expedition to the gulf of Las Hibueras, sixty thousand ounces of gold

were sent to your Majesty's treasury, the bearers being
Diego de Ocampo and Francisco Montejo; and if a greater
sum was not then sent, it was merely owing to the orders
issued in your Majesty's Council of the Indies respecting
the gold to be sent from these parts to Spain, it being my
private opinion and that of your Majesty's officers also, that
in remitting so large an amount of gold we somewhat exceeded ourselves, and contravened the laws promulgated
on the subject. Knowing, however, the stress in which your
Majesty was at the time for want of money, we determined
on making the said remittance, and I for my part sent to
your Majesty every thing I had in the world, including a
field piece entirely made of silver, which cost me in metal,
working, and other expenses, upwards of thirty-five thousand ounces of gold. This I sent by a servant of mine,
Diego de Soto by name, as well as certain Indian ornaments,
jewels, and gems, which, independently of their value, were
dear to me as memorials of the conquest; but as the French
took possession of those sent in the first instance, and I was
grieved to hear that your Majesty had not cast your eyes on
them, I sent every thing I possessed of the kind, not re-
serving even one single gold ounce, that your Majesty might
see a specimen, however trifling, of the workmanship and
civilisation of these Indians. It being, therefore, quite
proved that my intentions have always been to serve your
Majesty with pure zeal and unbounded submission, and to present with due humility everything of mine, I cannot see how
I can be accused of having defrauded your Majesty of your
rights and monies. I have likewise been told that during my
absence the officers entrusted with the government of this
country have occasionally sent sums of money to Spain, so
that, in truth, whenever there has been an opportunity, re-
mittances from these distant regions have never failed.

I have, in a similar manner, been informed, most powerful
lord, that some of my enemies have written to your Majesty

about the profits I derive from the provinces allotted to me, pretending that I have an income of two hundred millions. To show the absurdity of such computation, and in order to prove to your Majesty my readiness for the royal service, and the truth of my assertions—a thing of all others which has been the constant aim of my life—I consent to make over to your Majesty the enormous rents which, according to report, I am said to possess. There can be no better opportunity for me to convince your Majesty of the truth and purity of my intentions, and therefore, from this moment, I do transfer to the royal treasury the whole of the above specified income. I hope to gain by so doing, especially as it may be the means of expelling any suspicion lurking in the royal mind, of which the people of this country seem to be publicly aware. I, therefore, humbly beseech your Majesty to accept the offer of everything I possess on this continent, and make me instead a donation of twenty millions in Spain. In this manner your Majesty will keep the remaining one hundred and eighty millions, and I shall live contented at the Imperial court, where, I presume, no one will surpass me in fidelity and devotion, or dare to shadow my services to the crown. Even as regards the affairs of this country, I fancy that I can be, whilst at court, of much use to your Majesty, because as an eye-witness, and one who knows the country well, I shall advise that which is most convenient for the royal interests, and prevent the councillors being deceived by false reports or representations from this country. And I can assure your Majesty that it will be no inconsiderable service that I shall render by coming into the royal presence, and advising of what is to be provided for the preservation and keeping of this conquered land, and for the conversion of the natives to our Catholic faith, and for the increase of your Majesty's revenue in these parts; for I have no doubt that by so doing it will go on increasing and not diminishing, as it has been the case in the islands and in Tierra Firme, for lack of good administration, and the Catholic kings, father and grandfather of your Majesty, not being properly counseled, but following the advice of persons who for their own particular interest misrepresented the state of things, as have done all those who have sent reports from these countries. What is the use, I ask, to conquer those extensive territories, and keep them until now, at such an expense and notwithstanding so many obstacles and difficulties, if what good was found in them is not properly fostered and increased?

Two things make me wish in particular that your Majesty should be good enough to call me to the royal presence. One, and the principal of the two, is in order to convince your Majesty and the world at large of my loyalty and fidelity to the imperial service, it being the thing which I most prize of all the advantages that might accrue to me in this world; for if I have exposed my person to so many fatigues and dangers, and have undergone such hardships, it was merely to gain the name of servant of your Majesty and of the imperial crown, and not for sheer covetousness and desire of treasure. Indeed, had I been inspired by such a sentiment, I should not have lavished and thrown away those I possessed—no inconsiderable allowance, indeed, for a poor gentleman like me—to forward that which I hold as my principal aim and object. My sins, however, have no doubt been the cause of my not obtaining that favour which I so much covet, nor do I believe that, placed as I am now in your Majesty's estimation, I really could vindicate my conduct and escape the shafts of my calumniators, unless the immense favour which I am now asking, should be granted to me.

From fear, however, that your Majesty may imagine that I ask too much, in order that my proposition be rejected—though the sum is hardly sufficient for my decent maintenance at court—I will be contented with ten millions of

yearly revenue. This would enable me to appear without
shame in your Majesty's presence, after having held in these
parts the reins of government in the royal name, having
so effectually and considerably increased the patrimonial
estates and dominions of your Majesty, placing under the
imperial sway so many provinces covered with important
towns and noble cities; rooting up and destroying so many
idolatries, which were a daily offence to our God and Creator;
bringing most of the inhabitants to the knowledge of our
true catholic faith, and so implanting the same in this land,
that, if there be no impediment on the part of those who think
ill of these matters, and direct their attention and their zeal
to other ends, it may be reasonably expected that within
a very short time a new church shall be raised in these
parts, where God, our Lord, will be better served and more
honoured than in any other church of this world.

I again declare that, if your Majesty be pleased to order
that ten millions should be consigned to me annually in those
realms, and that, this being granted, I may come to your
Majesty's presence and serve at court, I will consider it as
a great favour, even leaving behind everything I here possess; for in so doing, my most sanguine hopes shall be
realised, and the wish of all my life, which is to serve at
the imperial court and under the eyes of your Majesty,
where my loyalty and fidelity may become manifest.

The other reason which I have for wishing to come to
your Majesty's presence, is this, that I may then be able to
give such information respecting the state of this country,
and even of the adjacent islands, as will tend to the better
service of God, our Lord, and of your catholic Majesty;
because I shall then be believed on such matters; whereas
treating them from here, my enemies are sure to say that I
write under the influence of passion, and am moved only by my
own personal interest, and not out of zeal for your Majesty's
service, and as your faithful vassal. Such is my desire of

kissing your Majesty's royal feet, and to serve at the imperial court, that I could not well describe it if I attempted, and therefore should your Majesty not be pleased to grant this, my humble request, or deem it inopportune to allot me the said yearly income for my maintenance at court, I beg and entreat that your Majesty will allow me to retain what I already possess in this country; or what my agents at court will ask for in my name, making it a perpetual pension for me and my heirs, so that I may not arrive in your Majesty's kingdom begging the people's alms. I shall consider it a great boon if your Majesty will send me permission to repair to those countries, and accomplish my said wish, for I trust in your Majesty's catholic conscience, that my services being made patent, as well as my pure intentions, your Majesty will not consent that I live in poverty.

I must add that the arrival of this judge of enquiry seemed to me a very good opportunity, and ample cause at the same time for the accomplishment of my said wish; and that I even began to make preparations for my journey, and would have departed had it not been for two reasons : one was my being at the time without money to spend on the way, my house in this city having been pillaged and robbed of all its contents; the other was my being afraid that during my absence from this country the natives might revolt, and the Spaniards get into quarrels, of both of which the experience of the past has made me apprehensive and cautious.

Whilst I was, most Catholic sir, drawing up this despatch for your Sacred Majesty, a messenger arrived from the South Sea, with letters informing me that on that coast, and not far from a place called Tecoantepec, a ship had anchored which, according to report, and the contents of another letter from her master, which I here enclose, belongs to the armada sent under Captain Loaysa to the Malucco Islands. As the said letter—of which I send the original—contains the parti-

culars and incidents of her voyage, I shall not stop to relate
them, but will only mention what I did on the occasion for the
better service of your Majesty. I immediately sent a com-
petent person to that place on the coast where the ship was,
with instructions, in case her master wished to go back to
Spain, to have him provided with everything he might want,
and learn from him the particulars of his voyage, the route
he had followed, and the observations he had made, so as to
send your Majesty a full report of the whole by the shortest
possible way. Calculating, moreover, that the ship might
want repairs, I sent thither a pilot to navigate her to the
port of Çacatula, where I have now three vessels of mine
ready to start on an exploring expedition to that sea and
coast, and I gave orders that she should be repaired and re-
fitted in the manner most suitable for your Majesty's service,
and the object of her voyage. As soon as the report arrives,
I shall not fail to forward it, in order that your Majesty may
be rightly informed, and tell us the royal pleasure respecting the said ship and her future destination.

My vessels in the South Sea, as I have already told
your Majesty, are in a fit state to undertake their voyage
of exploration, because on my first arrival in this capital,
after my expedition to the gulph of Las Hibueras, I began
to make in all haste the necessary preparations. They would
already have left the port had it not been that I expected
from Spain certain arms, artillery, and ammunition which
I had ordered for them, and have since arrived. I hope to
God that, for your Majesty's good fortune and better service,
the said voyage shall be made and accomplished; for, even
if no strait is found, I feel confident that a way will be discovered in those parts, whereby your Majesty may be yearly
informed of what is done at the Especeria. And if your
Majesty should be pleased to grant me those mercies which
I asked for in certain capitulation respecting that discovery,
I offer myself to discover and conquer all the Especeria and

other islands, if there be any, between the Malucco, Malacca, and China, and so arrange matters that the spices and drugs, instead of being obtained through barter and exchange—as the King of Portugal has them now—may become your Majesty's exclusive property, and the inhabitants of those distant islands made to acknowledge the imperial sway. For I engage myself, in case the above grants be made to me, to go thither personally or send at my own expense such an armada as will subdue those countries and islands, and to people them with Spaniards, build fortresses, and so furnish them with artillery and war-stores, that they may be easily defended from the native princes, or any other that should attempt to invade them. I have no doubt that if your Majesty be pleased that I take charge of this affair, every thing will turn out as I say for your Majesty's better service; and as a proof of my sincerity, I consent, if such be not the case, to be punished for my rashness, and as one who tells his king an untruth.

I have, in like manner, after my arrival in this capital, occupied myself in sending by sea and land a number of Spaniards to settle on the banks of the Tabasco river, also called Grijalba, and conquer many provinces in that neighbourhood, whereby God, our Lord, and your Majesty will be served, and the ships navigating those seas much benefited. For the port is a good one, and if it is populated by Spaniards, and the natives in the vicinity are pacified, the vessels going to and fro will be secure, whereas nowadays all those that are cast on shore have their crews murdered by the savage Indians who live on the coast.

I am now sending also to the land of the Zapotecas three companies of men to invade it by three different places, so as to conquer and reduce it in the shortest possible period of time. The conquest, if achieved, will be very beneficial, not only on account of the evils which those people inflict daily upon the peaceable Indians in their vicinity; but also because they happen to possess and occupy the richest mining districts in the whole of New Spain, whence, once conquered, your Majesty is to derive considerable profit.

In a like manner I have decided to send an expedition to settle on the banks of the river of Las Palmas, lower down than the Panuco, to the north, in the direction of Florida; because I am told that the land there is good, and there is a seaport. Active preparations are being made for that campaign, and already the people who are to go have assembled in numbers, and I hope that God, our Lord's, and your Majesty's service shall there be promoted, the country being in every respect very fine.

Between the northern coast and the province of Mechuacan lies a certain nation of Indians, known by the name of Chichimecas. They are a barbarous people, and by no means so intelligent as the Indians of these parts. I now send in that direction sixty horse and two hundred foot, with a considerable number of the natives, our friends, that they may unravel the mysteries of that country and its inhabitants. Should they find them susceptible of civilisation, and capable of living as these others do, of arriving at a knowledge of our faith, and showing readiness for your Majesty's service, their instructions are to make every possible effort towards bringing them peaceably and by mild means under your Majesty's yoke, and to settle in that part of their country which appears most fit for it. If, on the contrary, the said Indians prove to be rebellious and disobedient, my people are directed to wage war upon them and make them slaves, in order that there may not remain in this land any thing or living creature that does not acknowledge your Majesty as a master, and is of use to the royal service; for, by making slaves of those barbarous nations—who live entirely in the condition of savages—I firmly believe that your Majesty will be served, and the Spaniards greatly benefited, as they will dig out gold, and perchance some of them, by living among us, will be converted and saved.

In the midst of those Chichimecas I am told that there is an extensive province very thickly populated, and covered with large towns, the inhabitants of which live in the same manner as the Mexican Indians. Some of their towns and villages have even been visited by Spaniards. I am confident that this will be their first settlement, as the country, I am told, abounds with silver mines.

Two months before my departure for the Gulf of Las Hibueras, most powerful sir, I despatched from this city to the town of Colima,[1] upon the South Sea, a distance of a hundred and four leagues, one of my captains with instructions to follow that coast downwards for about a hundred and fifty or two hundred leagues, and ascertain the nature of it, and see whether there were any ports. My captain did as he was ordered; he went for a hundred and thirty leagues inland, and brought me an account and description of several ports he had seen on the coast—a service of no small importance, considering the scarcity of harbours known in those seas. He also brought me notice of many very large towns where he had been, and of several numerous and warlike Indian tribes, with whom he had encounters, or who were peaceably subdued, and he did not go further, because he had but a small force with him, and could not procure forage for his horses. Among the news reported by that captain was that of a very considerable river, which the natives told him was ten days' march from the furthest point he reached, and about which and the people inhabiting its banks, they told him wonderful things. I am now about sending him again to those parts, with a larger force and better arms and ammunition, that he may reconnoitre that river, which, owing to the volume of its waters, its breadth and size, might well turn out to be a strait communicating

[1] One of the copies has Coliman.

with the two seas. As soon as he returns, I shall not fail to apprise your Majesty of the information he brings.

Every one of the captains above alluded to, is on the point of starting on the expedition for which he is intended. May God be pleased to guide them in a manner that may be serviceable to Him and to your Majesty. For my own part, I can only add, that I shall never cease to devote myself to the imperial service, even if certain to incur your Majesty's further displeasure; for the time will come when my faithful services shall be owned and recognised, and if that should not be, I am well contented with doing my duty, and knowing that all the world is aware of the fidelity with which I have served. This conviction is enough for me, and I wish no other inheritance for my children.

Most invincible sovereign, may God our Lord preserve for many years the life, and increase the power, of your sacred Majesty. From this city of Tenuxtitlan, on the 3rd day of September of 1526.

HERNANDO CORTES.